No. 46–
STEVE BIKO

by

Hilda Bernstein

International Defence & Aid Fund
104 Newgate Street, London EC1
April 1978

The International Defence and Aid Fund for Southern Africa has the following objects:-

1. To aid, defend and rehabilitate the victims of unjust legislation and oppressive and arbitrary procedures;

2. To support their families and dependants;

3. To keep the conscience of the world alive to the issues at stake.

ISBN No. 0 904759 21 0

Contents

		Page
I	Introduction	5
II	The Life of Steve Biko	8
III	Black Consciousness	11
IV	The Death of Steve Biko	19
V	The Funeral	25
VI	The Inquest	28
VII	The Police	34
VIII	The Pathologists	66
IX	The Doctors	76
X	Counsel's Submission on Behalf of the Biko Family	98
XI	The Verdict	115
XII	Unanswered Questions	118
XIII	The Courts	127
XIV	Postscript	135
	References	136
	Appendix A	137
	Appendix B	148
	Illustrations	following 75

I

This is the year which people will talk about
This is the year which people will be silent about.

The old see the young die.
The foolish see the wise die.

The earth no longer produces, it devours.
The sky hurls down no rain, only iron.   *Bertolt Brecht*

Steve Biko died on 12 September, 1977. It was as though he had been a pebble
flung into a pool; the circles spread out and out, until ripples touched far shores.
He was the forty-sixth political detainee known to have died under interrogation by the security police in South Africa since the first 'no-trial' detention laws
were introduced in 1963. Since his death, two more detainees—one only 18
years old—have died in detention.

In not a single case has an independent inquiry been held; nor has any member
of the security police or anyone else been held responsible for the killings. Death
takes place while the victim is within a closed circle that cannot be penetrated
by friends or relatives. The evidence of how each one died can only be given by
those within this circle, or by professional interpretation of the marks and injuries
on the corpse—the silent witness.

But Steve Biko's story attracted world-wide attention that has not, in the past,
been focused on these other deaths. Black leaders, even those well-known to
black people within South Africa, are seldom known to the rest of the world.
They have no means of becoming known: they are outside the range of the media,
without a press and without access to radio or television. Their organisations are
illegal or operate semi-legally, often fragmented and local because of the size of
South Africa and the prohibitions on political activities. Individuals who do
become known are swiftly eliminated from the public eye by bans that silence
them, confine them to small areas, and prohibit them from meeting anybody or
being quoted anywhere. Their names, often difficult to remember, sink into the
obscurity of legal proscriptions.

Steve Biko was different. Educated, intellectual, articulate, he was not only
founder of and a leader in the Black Consciousness movement but he became
more widely-known to members of the powerful and privileged white minority
in South Africa. He had met United States senators and embassy officials. He
had a friend who was a newspaper editor. Although for some time before his
death he had been restricted to his home town under a banning order and unable
to travel, many people came to see him. He had become known beyond the immediate circle of workers and students who shared his organisations and his ideas.

Clearly he had those attributes that combine to make an impression. His friends describe him as handsome, fearless, a brilliant thinker. Denis Herbstein, a journalist who came from the same town as Biko, wrote: 'In a country where violence by the State and its police is endemic, Biko managed to remain non-violent, although his more youthful supporters urged him to go on the offensive. But he was ready to defend himself. While in solitary confinement a police interrogator got rough with him. Biko punched the man on the head. He was treated more correctly after that and released three months later to tell the tale'.[1]

Biko's importance was developed as a leader of black people; but it was through the white press and white friends that people outside South Africa first heard of him. Without them, however deeply mourned by those among whom he had worked, he would have been just one more statistic, the forty-sixth detainee known to have died while in detention. A disregarded black man.

From among the other forty-five, it is possible to take any name and find there a story as poignant as that of Steve Biko. There was Alpheus Maliba, for instance, a Venda from the Northern Transvaal. He was different from Biko, an uneducated peasant who came to Johannesburg and taught himself about life and politics in the bitter school of the super-exploited blacks, as an unskilled, under-paid worker. He became a trade unionist, a peasant leader, and an organiser. He was no longer a young man when the organisations he belonged to were banned and his activities proscribed; he dropped out of political activity, and returned to the Northern Transvaal to earn a living.

One day there was a small announcement in a newspaper: detainee found hanged. Nobody in Johannesburg knew he had been detained, nor for how long; nobody knew how he actually died and few, other than those who had worked with him in the past, even knew Alpheus Maliba was dead.

The tally of these deaths in detention began slowly, two or three a year. Towards the end of the 1960's the pace accelerated. Most of them attracted little attention although the deaths seemed mysterious and the curt announcements—'found hanged' or 'natural causes'—inadequate. There would be a small paragraph in a newspaper; or nothing.

In other cases public attention was aroused by an inquest with disturbing evidence; harrowing details of broken and bruised bodies, of copper deposits left on the skin by electrodes, of multiple injuries that could not have occurred in the way the police maintained. Rarely, the victim was widely known, as in the case of the Imam Abdullah Haron whose death from multiple injuries stirred the Malay community in the Cape where he had been a loved and respected leader. Or the circumstances aroused particular disquiet, as when the young teacher, Ahmed Timol, was said to have committed suicide by jumping from the window of a tenth-floor room while being interrogated—a room that was sound-proof, escape-proof and had barred windows.

But most of the victims, from 1963 onwards, died in silence and secrecy. Sometimes even their own families were not informed; often they would be buried before anyone knew about the death; or a post-mortem might be held hurriedly before an independent pathologist could be obtained.

6

From March, 1976, the number of deaths in detention began to mount; the explanations given by the police seemed more and more offhand or unlikely, or went contrary to known facts. In a year, 19 detainees died: in the next six months, four more.

Yet until the case of Steve Biko, the outside world scarcely heard or noted, although in January, 1977 the London *Times* had an editorial headed SECRET DEATH IN SOUTH AFRICA'S PRISONS which baldly stated that so low had the reputation of justice in South Africa fallen that only an international inquiry into deaths in detention would be acceptable. 'Default must be entered as an admission of guilt'.[2]

So always these others must be remembered. Sometimes, however, it is possible to see the structure of a whole nation through the life and death of one person. Perhaps it is easier to see it this way. People are 'shocked' in a conventional sense to read that a minimum of forty-six South Africans have died in detention in the last few years. But they are moved to the very depths of their being by the thought of one man, naked and manacled, driven 740 miles through the night as he lay unattended and dying.

There are many questions to be answered. How did Biko receive the injury that caused his death? Who inflicted it, under what circumstances? Why was he kept naked and chained? Why did the doctors who attended him fail to interpret the undisputed signs of brain injury? Why did the doctors and all the police who were with him from the time he was injured until he died, all fail to notice the wound on his forehead which is so clearly visible in photos taken after his death?

And even more: why was the brain-damaged and dying man finally sent off on the long, terrible drive to Pretoria—from Port Elizabeth, a big city with adequate hospitals? Why did the police give conflicting evidence, often caught out in contradictory statements or outright lies, none of which could explain the head injury? They had the time and the ability to concoct a story that would, at least superficially, account for the wound on Biko's head. Why did they not do so? Why was an inquest held, why were details of the way he was treated permitted to be broadcast to the world. Why did the inquest find that no one was responsible for his death?

As the story of his arrest and death unfolds, bit by bit, through cross-examination at the inquest, the answers to some of these questions begin to emerge. Until finally the questions to be answered centre around the role of the courts themselves in South Africa, and on how deep the corruption of life and morality has penetrated in the apartheid state.

Stephen Biko is our magnifying glass. Through him and his fate a whole spectrum of South African reality is exposed. Perhaps it was always visible; but now it comes sharply into focus. What was confusing is clarified. What was obscure is revealed. In the fate of Steve Biko is encapsulated the truth about South Africa today, and the truth about its twenty-six million citizens, four-fifths black and one-fifth white.

II

The Life of Steve Biko

Stephen Bantu Biko was born in King William's Town, in the Cape Province of South Africa, in 1946. After matriculating he went to Natal University to study medicine in 1966.

Initially he involved himself in the activities of the National Union of South African Students (NUSAS), but he and others felt increasingly that NUSAS was dominated by white liberals. In 1968 the all-black South African Students' Organisation (SASO) was formed with Biko as its first president.

'When we broke away to form an exclusive black movement', Biko stated, 'we were accused of being anti-white. But with many more whites at university, the non-racial students' union was dominated by white liberals. They made all the decisions for us. We needed time to look at our own problems, and not leave them to people without experience of the terrible conditions in the black townships or of the system of Bantu education'.[3]

Together with other SASO office-bearers Biko travelled the country, visiting black campuses and propounding the emergent philosophy of black consciousness. They defined 'black' as including not only Africans, but Coloured (mixed-race) and Indians—all those designated 'non-white' by the apartheid state.

At the end of his third year at university he was expelled for his political activities. He was under constant surveillance and harassment from the security police. But in the same year he was instrumental in forming the Black Peoples' Convention (BPC), as an umbrella political movement for groups sharing the ideas of 'Black Consciousness'.

In 1972 Biko started working for the Black Community Programmes in Durban; among its projects was *Black Review* 1972, an analysis of political trends. *Black Review* was subsequently banned, and in February 1973 Biko himself, together with other officials of SASO and BPC, was served with banning orders.

Banning orders are designed severely to restrict the activities and lives of those on whom they are served. Biko was immediately banned from all the organisations with which he had been associated, and he was restricted to King William's Town for the next five years—that is, he was not permitted to leave the confines of the town. A banned person is also prohibited from being at any meeting, and a meeting takes place as soon as the banned person talks to two people together. This meant that not only could Biko no longer work in the organisations he had helped to found, but he could not meet to have discussions with others. Friends could come to visit him, provided only one person came at a time, and provided they themselves were not banned. (Banned people may not communicate with other banned people.)

Banned people also may not write for publication, nor may anything they say be quoted. There are other restrictions placed on banned people, usually prohibiting them from entering various buildings, such as any court, educational institutions, the offices of newspapers and other publishers, and similar places. Biko was also refused a passport to attend a conference to which he had been invited by the Catholic Justice and Peace Commission in Germany.

Life for a banned person is full of tensions and requires constant alertness. The homes of banned people are normally visited frequently by the security police. If Biko were to be in a room with his wife at a time when a friend walked in, he was liable to be arrested for breaking his bans. In fact the banned person must become his own jailer. But because bans require a total withdrawal from all social and political activities, a total retirement from any involvement, many banned people seek ways to work in spite of the difficulties.

Biko's restrictions only increased his determination to work among his own people. He knew the needs of the black community, and he believed in self-help. In 1975 he founded the Zimele Trust Fund to help political prisoners and their families, and the Ginsberg Educational Trust for the purpose of assisting black students.

In that same year the government acted against the young black militants by taking many into detention. Biko was one of those arrested; he was held for 137 days without charge or trial.

Restrictions on him were increased at the end of the year, when he was prohibited even from associating with the Black Community Programme. But he still managed to do some work. He became Secretary-General of the Zimele Trust Fund in 1976, and in that year, at the congress of the Black People's Convention in Durban—a congress he could not attend because of his banning orders—Biko was elected Honorary President of the organisation.

Thus Biko remained active despite the many bans, and his prestige, particularly among young activists, was high. During the disturbances following the police massacre of Soweto students in June 1976 Soweto leaders demanded that the government negotiate the country's future with three black leaders—Nelson Mandela, leader of the African National Congress, imprisoned for life on Robben Island; the late Robert Sobukwe, leader of the Pan Africanist Congress, living under restrictions in Kimberley; and Steve Biko.

Biko was arrested and detained many times. He was first charged with breaking his banning orders in 1974; he was acquitted. Thereafter he was arrested and charged several times on different counts, including various allegations that he had broken his banning orders and a charge of obstructing the course of justice by persuading witnesses in a political trial to change their evidence.

In August 1976, at a time of mass demonstrations against apartheid throughout the country following the Soweto massacres, Biko was arrested together with a reporter from the East London *Daily Dispatch*; he was held in solitary confinement for 101 days. His bans prevented any statement or account of his detention from being published.

Once again, in March 1977, he was arrested, detained, then later released. And again in July 1977, arrested, charged and released on bail.

Arising out of the revolt of school children against Bantu Education that began in Soweto in July 1976, many pupils and students, their ages ranging from 17 to 24 years, had been arrested in Port Elizabeth and charged under the security laws with conspiring to commit sabotage, and to hinder the police during demonstrations. In one case, 31 students were each sentenced to five years' imprisonment.

When Biko was arrested in July, 1977, it was on a charge of defeating the ends of justice in a case involving other school students. The State claimed that Biko had instructed seven students to say they were forced to make false statements to the police. In his judgment the magistrate found the evidence given by the accused 'was certainly far more satisfactory than that of the State witnesses'. There were cries of *Amandla!* (Power) and clenched fists salutes from the crowded public gallery in the court when Biko was discharged.[4]

Some charges against Biko were still pending at the time of his death, including one of breaking his banning order when he entered an educational institution to write an examination (he was studying law by correspondence), but Biko was never convicted of any crime while he lived. He was never arrested for inciting violence, never accused of it. The police waited until he was dead to make their wild accusations. Then they said they had documents to prove Biko was a terrorist, planning sabotage, murder, riots in the streets. 'They do not accuse people—they accuse documents', wrote Donald Woods. 'I could write documents myself and say that the Prime Minister had just become a card-carrying member of the Communist Party'.[5]

Finally, August 1977. Biko was arrested once again. Together with a friend and BPC activist, Peter Jones, he was stopped in a car at a roadblock and taken into custody in Port Elizabeth.

The fate of Peter Jones is not known. At the time of writing, he is still in detention.

III

Black Consciousness

What had Steve Biko done to be so persecuted by the police? Why did they pursue him so persistently and find him so dangerous, when no charges had been proved against him? It was as though his very existence was regarded as threatening the stability of the apartheid state, and the state turned the formidable strength of its restrictive laws and its powerful security police to eradicate this threat.

Biko was persecuted as a leading exponent of Black Consciousness, the mixture of ideas and action which emerged in the early 1970's with the aim of uniting black people to oppose apartheid and white supremacy. As such he was seen as a threat.

Whatever their differences with some of the principles of their forerunners, the Black Consciousness movement was descended from the organisations that the government banned in 1960, following the police massacre of peaceful demonstrators at Sharpeville—the African National Congress and the Pan Africanist Congress.

The ANC and PAC went underground and into exile. Using techniques and personnel taught by experts in the USA and Portugal, the security police waged a relentless war against African organisations and all their former members and supporters, who had been identified, listed and marked down in the years when the organisations had operated legally up to 1960.

The mid 1960's were a period during which the political aspirations of the people of South Africa appeared to be totally silenced. There was a series of devastating trials of which the best-known was the 'Rivonia' trial, when leaders of the African National Congress (Nelson Mandela, Walter Sisulu, Govan Mbeki and others) were sent to Robben Island for the rest of their natural lives. Trials in many different parts of the country continued for a long period. It seemed the old organisations had been broken up and totally suppressed. Revival waited on a new generation.

In the late 1960's and early 1970's new organisations began to take shape, in the first place among black students. SASO (South African Students Organisation) soon spread through the segregated black universities—the 'tribal colleges' —although its militancy was not welcomed by the authorities. The movement grew among black intellectuals, journalists and poets and stimulated creativity in poetry and the theatre.

The Policy Manifesto adopted by SASO at its 2nd General Students' Council in July 1971 defines its concept of Black Consciousness.[6] SASO believes, it states, that South Africa is a country in which both black and white live and shall continue to live together. But that, because of privileges accorded to them by law and because of their continued maintenance of an oppressive regime, whites must be excluded from the struggle towards realising black aspirations.

The idea of Black Consciousness and the organisations which it inspired are themselves direct products of bans and prohibitions, of the whole apartheid regime. The concept of Black Consciousness was not a new one devised by Biko that thrust itself suddenly on the South African scene. Nor did it derive directly from the 'Black Power' movement in the USA, as the government tried to claim. And the emphasis on black nationalism was not a new and hitherto unknown proposition.

National unity of Africans, founded on national consciousness, was the first aim of the ANC from its inception in 1912. The idea was propounded more forcefully by the ANC Youth League, formed in 1943 by a younger generation of potential leaders, impatient of the tactics of petitions and pleas of the past. The new group accepted the general policies and goals of the ANC, but sought to generate among the African masses a spirit of militant nationalism and self-reliance.

In 1946 A. M. Lembede prepared a policy document for the ANC Youth League[7] in which he rejected co-operation between Africans and other groups. While this might be highly desirable, he said, it could only take place between Africans organised as a single unit and other 'non-European' groups as separate units. 'Non-European unity is a fantastic dream which has no foundation in reality'.

Lembede spoke of the pathological state of mind brought about among blacks by racism—the loss of self-confidence, inferiority complex, frustration, and idolisation of whites. Lembede died young, but some of the strands from the ideas he propounded were taken up by the Pan-Africanist Congress when it split away from the ANC at the end of 1958. (PAC rejected co-operation with other groups and emphasised black nationalism. It believed in an 'Africanist' struggle for liberation.) Other elements in the Youth League developed from this early 'nationalist' position to a revolutionary position in which they were prepared to fight with people of all races.

In 1948 the ANC Youth League Manifesto described African nationalism as 'the dynamic national liberatory creed of the oppressed African people'. It sought to create 'a united nation out of heterogeneous tribes, free Africans from foreign domination and enable Africa to make her own contribution to human progress and happiness'.[8]

Black Consciousness emerged again as a potent idea in a period when despite the rejection of tribalism by all strands of the liberation movement in the past and their emphasis on black unity, separate development was being applied forcibly as government policy through many laws; through the Group Areas Act, which provides for total residential separation of different racial groups; through separate 'tribal' colleges—part of the whole scheme of Bantu Education; through separate political parties ('mixed-race' organisations became illegal).

Thus the first aim of Black Consciousness was to conquer feelings of black inferiority, to inculcate black pride. Black Consciousness was declared a way of life, an attitude of mind, with the basic tenet that the black man must reject all value systems that seek to make him a foreigner in the country of his birth and reduce his basic human dignity. It implied awareness by black people of the power they wield, both economically and politically; and that the black man must build his own value system, see himself as self-defined and not defined by others: 'Liberation of the black man begins first with liberation from psychological oppression by himself through an inferiority complex'.[9]

Much emphasis was placed on Black Consciousness as a state of mind. And Black Consciousness also contained a strong element of Christianity.

Out of the movement grew a new wave of cultural energy expressed particularly in drama and poetry:

I
am the liberator
no
white man can liberate me
only
a black man can free himself.

The poetry of lament gave way to the poetry of liberation, a positive, proud, defiant expression of being black:

Tame a mamba
Set it to work and starve it
Teach it your language
And when it speaks, lock it in.

Tame a mamba
Teach it your culture
And mock it
Restrict its movements
Find it outside at night, arrest it
And when it hibernates
Search for it and send it to jail.

Tame a mamba
But when it resists
And begins to hiss
Send it to the gallows.[10]

13

While SASO specifically excluded whites, a resolution of the Black Renaissance Convention held at Hammanskraal in December 1974 rejected all forms of racism and discrimination. It called for a united and democratic South Africa, and an anti-racist society.

However, perhaps partly because it sought to operate openly and legally, the Black Consciousness movement became less definite when defining its objectives. Drake Koka, first secretary of the BPC, described his organisation as 'not a movement of confrontation, but a movement of introspection'.[11] And Adam Small, a leading poet and writer and spokesman on Black Consciousness said 'Protest itself is a form of begging, really, and we have indeed decided that we are no longer going to beg white South Africa . . . Instead we are simply to manifest our pride in Blackness time and time again'.[12]

As the liberation movements banned by the government were committed to an armed and underground struggle, the Black Consciousness movement took on the role of 'overground', trying to operate within the laws, and preferring to work through community projects. (It was strongly committed to self-help schemes such as clinics). Inevitably more militant attitudes were expressed by many within the movement.

Biko refuted the liberal idea of integration as a counter to apartheid because it was impossible to achieve. The whole system had to be overhauled before black and white could walk together hand in hand to oppose a common enemy. He wrote:

'While the white liberal identifies with the blacks, the burden of the enormous privileges which he still uses and enjoys becomes lighter. Yet at the back of his mind is a constant reminder that he is quite comfortable as things stand and therefore should not bother about change'.[13]

The thesis of white racism, according to Biko, could only have one valid antithesis: a solid black unity to counter-balance the scale. 'If South Africa is to be a land where black and white live in harmony without fear of group exploitation, it is only when these two opposites have interplayed and produced a viable synthesis of ideas and *modus vivendi*. We can never wage any struggle without offering a strong counterpoint to the white racism that permeates our society so effectively'.

Biko believed that no group, however benevolent, could hand power to the vanquished on a plate. "We must accept that the limits of tyrants are prescribed by the endurance of those whom they oppress . . . our situation is not a mistake on the part of whites but a deliberate act, and no amount of moral lecturing will persuade the white man to 'correct' the situation".

In many ways, Biko's exposition of Black Consciousness echoed ideas from the past, such as Lembede's. But while Lembede had emphasised the exclusion of all non-Africans, Biko expounded the unity of all those who were discriminated against on the grounds of colour or race, and thus Black Consciousness embraced the Coloured and Indian sections of the population as well as the African.

Other echoes from Lembede emerges in Biko's ideas. For example, Lembede asserted that blacks, while retaining and preserving belief in the 'immortality of our dead ancestors', must base their present-day ethical system on Christian morals. Thirty years later, Biko spoke of the need to re-assess history and give past leaders of the blacks their true place; while there was a strong case for a re-examination of Christianity: 'I do not wish to question the basic truth at the heart of the Christian message".

'Out of the heterogeneous tribes', declared Lembede, 'there must emerge a homogeneous nation . . . the feeling of being Africans irrespective of tribal connections, social status, educational attainment or economic class'. Biko, thirty years on, called for blacks to resist all attempts by protagonists of the Bantustan theory to fragment them: 'We are oppressed, not as individuals, not as Zulus, Xhosas, Vendas, or Indians. We are oppressed because we are black. We must use that very concept to unite ourselves and to respond as a cohesive group'.[14]

Steve Biko refuted charges that Black Consciousness was a parallel type of black racism. Merely by describing yourself as black, he said, you have started on a road towards emancipation, you have committed yourself to fight against all forces that seek to use your blackness as a stamp that marks you out as a subservient human being.

Biko was always a spokesman for 'non-violent' ways. This emphasis was one reason why Steve Biko and Black Consciousness won some acceptance amongst white South African liberals, and a measure of support from statesmen of the Western world. But there is not, nor can ever be, a 'non-violent' situation in today's South Africa. The laws themselves are violent laws, violently administered (what better witness to that than Biko's own death?). There may be pauses between the eruptions of violent confrontation in the townships and on the streets; but they mark only the ebb and flow of the constant underlying and overt violence.

In their dealing with blacks the police are not bound by Christian ethics but by the precepts of power, in which might is right. There is no way in which action against apartheid starting from the most peaceful forms of protest can be kept within the framework laid down by the leaders. Even in the early days, SASO confrontations with state authorities on campuses of the tribal colleges soon became violent. SASO leader O. R. Abram Tiro was assassinated by a parcel bomb when he fled to Botswana in 1974. Inevitably the apartheid state would move violently against the growing organisations, against the articulate young intellectuals who wrote stinging poems and pilloried the white-run state. It awaited only the occasion. The occasion was decided when SASO/BPC organised a series of rallies in support of the victory of FRELIMO in Mozambique.

The events in Mozambique and later in Angola struck South Africans with tremendous force. If whites, at first totally unbelieving, felt tremors of fear at the shattering defeat of their armed intervention in Angola, blacks greeted the

15

end of Portuguese colonial rule and the triumph of the liberation organisations with tremendous joy.

SASO and BPC decided to 'share in the joy of the FRELIMO victory'; the struggles in South Africa and in Mozambique 'are clearly intertwined', they claimed, for their common purpose is 'the realisation of a free and united Africa —the birthplace and mother country of the black peoples of the world'.[15]

As soon as the rallies were publicized, the Minister of Police invoked special powers to ban all gatherings throughout South Africa. Despite the ban, large crowds gathered at Currie's Fountain in Durban and at the University of the North, Turfloop (one of the tribal colleges). Police moved in with dogs, batons and tear gas. The crowds were attacked and dispersed. SASO offices were raided, representatives of both organisations arrested. Harassment, arrests, confiscation of typewriters, documents and other materials, continued for two weeks. The end-product a trial—which came to be called the SASO-BPC trial.

It was the longest trial that had yet been heard under the Terrorism Act. The *Rand Daily Mail* described it as a trial of Black Consciousness itself. There were 136 days in court, 61 state witnesses, 21 defence witnesses. All nine accused, together with other members of SASO and BPC, had been kept in detention without charge under Section 6 of the Terrorism Act for periods of up to 130 days before their first court appearance in January 1975. They were kept in custody during the whole of the trial period. Almost 16 months of jail, much of it spent in solitary confinement, before they were sentenced.

One of the reasons for the length of the trial was that though 'terrorism' was charged, no actual act of physical terrorism or of recruitment for military training was alleged by the State. The issue in the trial was whether 'black consciousness' as a philosophy, and as practised by the two organisations, constituted 'terrorism'. The indictment was concerned with speeches and pamphlets issued between 1971 and 1974, showing, so the State alleged, that the accused had conspired to commit acts which would bring revolutionary change to South Africa; and had been involved in 'a course of preparation' to recruit blacks into a Black Power bloc hostile to whites and to the state.

In the week before Christmas in 1976, white South Africans were preparing for lavish spending while black South Africans were observing a period of mourning for the many who had died in confrontations with the South African police in the six months which began in Soweto in June. And in the Palace of Justice, in Pretoria, Mr. Justice Boshoff passed sentence on nine exponents of Black Consciousness—six of the accused to six years' imprisonment, the other three to five years.

'In our country', said Mr. Justice Boshoff, 'we have democratic regime norms, and freedom of speech and assembly play an important part in our party system, which is based on opposing views and consequent dispute of ideas. . . While freedom of speech and assembly must be regarded as fundamental in our demo-

16

cratic society, it does not mean that everyone with opinions or beliefs to express may address a group at any public place and at any time'.

He recognised that blacks had no effective voice or vote in the allocation of values and could only protest against 'what might be regarded by them as grievances', and was satisfied that neither SASO nor BPC had the characteristics of a revolutionary group. But he felt that the concept of Black Consciousness, in building group cohesion and solidarity, did encourage feelings of hostility between blacks and whites. In what must be one of the most significant judgements in South African legal history he accordingly convicted the nine accused as 'terrorists' on the basis that they had expressed the political frustrations and attitudes of the blacks in South Africa, and more particularly of the Black Consciousness movement. A precedent had thus been created. *Terrorism may now be committed not only through physical violence, but also through the expression of thoughts, ideas and desires for liberation.* And to characterise the white power system as one of murder, oppression, exploitation, fascism, robbery, or plunder is now 'an act of terrorism'.

By the time these judgements were given, Steve Biko was already restricted and confined to King William's Town, which is why he had not been indicted with the others who had been put on trial. Now some of his fellow Black Consciousness leaders were in prison, and many had been forced, like so many before them, into exile.

The Minister and the police, by restricting Biko so severely, had enabled him to escape trial. But they had not stopped him from continuing to play a role in the Black Consciousness movement. Despite the ferocity of repression the unrest that began with the students of Soweto was continuing. Boycotts against the schools were widespread, and many of them were in the Eastern Cape and in the Ciskei area close to King William's Town.

As long as Biko still remained alive he was a dangerous enemy of apartheid. His image was untarnished; his prestige among black Africans was high; and he commanded respect among those whites with whom he had come into contact.

With the SASO/BPC 'terrorists' contained, the security police turned their attention to the destruction of this potent leader. The official government and police view was that unrest was not endemic among blacks, but the direct result of 'agitators'. This meant not simply restraining those designated as agitators, but publicly proving that they had conducted 'agitation' or planned 'terrorist' activities.

It was not enough just to detain Biko under Section 6. It was not enough to prefer charges, if they could be made. After many years, even decades, of imprisonment on Robben Island, black prisoners, once released, plunged back again into political activity. And the images of those remaining on the Island were still powerful.

It was in this context that Steve Biko faced the last few months of his life.

17

The Terrorism Act (Section 6)

The Terrorism Act (No. 83 of 1967) establishes the offence of 'participation in terrorist activities', such activities being very broadly defined. Furthermore, if an accused is found guilty of having committed any act included in the list, the onus is on him to prove that his intention was not to commit terrorism. Once convicted, the minimum sentence that the court may impose is 5 years' imprisonment, the maximum—death.

Section 6 of the Terrorism Act allows any officer of the police over a certain rank to order the arrest without warrant, and the detention for interrogation, of any person whom he has reason to believe is a terrorist, or is withholding information relating to terrorists or to offences under the Act. A person so detained will be held, subject to such conditions as the Commissioner of Police or the Minister of Justice may determine, until the Commissioner is satisfied that he has replied adequately to all questions asked at his interrogation, or that no useful purpose will be served by his further detention, or until the Minister orders his release.

It could be added, in view of the number of deaths in detention under the Terrorism Act—"or until he dies".

The Act also provides that *no court of law may pronounce upon the validity of any action taken under the provisions relating to detention, nor order the release of any detainee.* No one shall have access to a detained person or be entitled to information about him except the Minister, or an officer of the State acting in his official capacity. If circumstances so permit, the detainee *may* be visited by a magistrate once a fortnight.

18

IV

The Death of Steve Biko

Biko was arrested for the last time on 18 August 1977 and detained under Section 6 of the Terrorism Act.

On 14 September, the *Rand Daily Mail* carried the report of his death:

Mr. Steve Biko, the 30-year-old black leader, widely regarded as the founder of the black consciousness movement in South Africa, died in detention on Monday (12th).

Mr. Biko, honorary president of the Black People's Convention and the father of two small children, is the 20th person to die in Security Police custody in 18 months.

The *Mail* report went on to quote a statement that the Minister of Justice, Mr. James Kruger, had issued the previous day:

Since 5 September Mr. Biko refused his meals and threatened to go on a hunger strike. He had been regularly supplied with meals and water, but refused to partake thereof.

On 7 September a district surgeon was called in because Mr. Biko appeared unwell. The district surgeon certified that he could find nothing wrong with Mr. Biko.

On 8 September the police again arranged for the district surgeon and the chief district surgeon to examine Mr. Biko and because they could diagnose no physical problem, they arranged that he be taken to the prison hospital for intensive examinations. On the same day he was examined by a specialist.

The following morning he was again examined by a doctor and kept at the hospital for observation.

On Sunday morning, 11 September, Mr. Biko was removed from the prison hospital to Walmer police station on the recommendation of the district surgeon. He still had not eaten on Sunday afternoon and again appeared unwell. After consultation with the district surgeon it was decided to transfer him to Pretoria. He was taken to Pretoria that same night.

On 12 September Mr. Biko was again examined by a district surgeon in Pretoria and received medical treatment. He died on Sunday night.*

This was an unusual statement. It is not customary for the Minister to comment on the death of a detainee, nor is it usual for details to be given con-

---

*12 September was in fact a Monday.

cerning a detainee's illness and doctors' visits. It seemed as though the Minister was trying to forestall any anticipated outcry about Biko's death.

But the statement raised more questions than it answered. The notion of a hunger strike, so out of keeping with Biko's response to persecution, was itself bizarre, and inevitably recalled other unlikely police explanations, as when Nichodimus Kgoathe was said to have died from broncho-pneumonia following head injuries allegedly sustained when he fell while taking a shower, or when Solomon Modipane died after having 'slipped on a piece of soap'.

Then, taking the story at its face value, how could a hunger strike of only six days by a person in good health and normal weight (Biko was, in fact, overweight) so speedily have resulted in death? That was quite incredible. And why, if nothing could be found physically wrong with him, was Biko examined by so many doctors, and removed to a hospital?

The statement contained one germ of truth when it said that on 7 September 'Mr. Biko appeared unwell'. This suggested—correctly as it turned out—that something happened on 7 September to make Biko 'unwell', hence all the subsequent examinations. The cause of his apparent ill-health became known at the post-mortem examination. For the time being the public could only suspect that the police version of a hunger strike, like so many explanations of detainees' deaths in the past, was an attempt to shift the blame for the death onto the detainee himself.

"His death leaves me cold" — *Minister of Police*

On 14 September Minister Kruger addressed a Nationalist Party Congress. To this he gave a larger and less formal, less restrained version, in his native Afrikaans[16]. He said:

I am not glad and I am not sorry about Mr. Biko. It leaves me cold (Dit laat my koud). I can say nothing to you. Any person who dies . . . I shall also be sorry if I die. (Laughter).

But now, there are a lot of scandal stories and all sorts of positions are now taken against the South African Police. And even if I am their Minister, Mr. Chairman, if they have done something wrong I shall be the first man to take them before the courts. They know it.

But what happened here? This person was arrested in connection with riots in Port Elizabeth. Among other things they were busy with the drafting and distribution of extremely inflammatory pamphlets which urged people to violence and arson.

Now I mention this fact, not because I want to criticise someone who is dead. I have respect for the dead. But I mention this fact to prove that we were justified in arresting this person . . .

On the 5 September they were finished with [the questioning of] the other man and then they came to him [Mr. Biko]. And they began to question him.

Then he said he would go on a hunger strike. He first said he would answer

20

their questions. They should give him a chance for a quarter of an hour. After a quarter of an hour, he said no, he would go on a hunger strike.

And indeed he began to push his food and water away—that were continually given to him so that he would freely eat or drink. It is very true what Mr. Venter [a congress delegate] said about prisoners in South Africa having the 'democratic right' to starve themselves to death. It is a democratic land.

We are now asked 'When you saw he went on hunger strike why didn't you force him to eat?' (Laughter).

Mr. Chairman, can you imagine that these same people who smear the police day and night because they touched this man—and there's a mark on his foot, and there's a mark on his ankle, and here's a mark behind his ear and it must be the police—do you think the police must still force that man to eat?

No Sir, I say now categorically on behalf of the police. If I was there I would have said, Do not touch him, but would have said, Call a doctor. . . .

That day the district surgeon came. On the 9 September the man still lay there on the mat. And then the police said: 'Don't just call the district surgeon, call the chief district surgeon. Let him come and look at this man'.

The first district surgeon wrote a letter to the detective to say 'There's nothing wrong with him'. The chief district surgeon and the district surgeon told the Security Police: 'Man, there is nothing wrong with this man'. . . .

Do you know what we brought in? We brought in a private specialist. We had a specialist with this man. We said, 'Look at this man'.

And on Sunday, 11 September, after we had had all those doctors and specialists, then the district surgeon said, 'Man, send him to one of the bigger hospitals'. . . .

[*Mr. Kruger then described how Steve Biko was brought to Pretoria Prison because there was a larger Prison Hospital there. And how that same night he was put in the care of the district surgeon.*]

Later that night—there is a peephole in these places, so that the people do not hang themselves . . .

Incidentally, I can just tell congress, the day before yesterday one of my own lieutenants in the prison service also committed suicide and we have not yet accused a single prisoner. (Laughter).

And when this man came to look in the peephole he saw that the man was lying very still. And he did not touch him and did not open the door. He did nothing. Because he also knows that if you touch him they say 'Your fingerprint is there, what did you do?' He left the man. I do not blame him. He went back and told a man: 'The man is lying dead still. There is something wrong'. And they summoned the doctor and they found the person was dead . . .

But, Sir, I just want to tell the congress and I want to tell the Press. I expect nothing from them [the press].

I know, Sir, I know because I have it in documents, that they are going for us.

They will search for nooks and crannies (gatjies en plekkies). Whether they will find them, I don't know. We are also only people.

But from my point of view, on the facts that I have, it looks to me as if what had to be done was done.

... I say to you as Minister, that I cannot see how we could have acted differently (Cheers and applause.)

Death in Detention — *Die Burger*

In an editorial[17] the government-supporting newspaper *Die Burger* said:

The death of detainees in South Africa is an emotional matter which generates much heat. But never before has it been as bad as in the latest case of the black power activist Steve Biko. Concern over detainees' deaths becomes deep dismay when the hysterical propaganda against authorities is observed...

A vehement campaign is in progress which surpasses all previous protests.

The venomous suggestions are of such an extravagant nature that it fills an objective observer with trepidation . . . The purpose is to discredit the security police . . .

The presumptuous condemnation is voiced on the grounds of unconfirmed suspicion, regardless of the fact that previous investigations have brought to light the fact that detainees frequently took their own lives or died of natural causes . . .

If deaths occur, it must be possible to prove ever more emphatically that it happened completely outside the control of the authorities.

It is imperative, for the sake of everyone's feeling of humaneness and justice, and for the sake of South Africa, which is being besmirched in such a terrible way.

Police have never been responsible for killing or torturing a single detainee — *South African Broadcasting Corporation, 16 September, 1977*

In a radio broadcast for abroad,[18] the SABC said:

The death of 30 year old Mr. Steve Biko while in detention appears to be receiving wide publicity but before people begin jumping the gun with condemnation it is necessary to consider the facts of the situation and not all of these have been disclosed as yet.

Mr. Biko, who can be regarded as a leader among certain radical black elements in the country, was arrested in mid-August. . . From 5 September he refused meals and threatened a hunger strike. [There follows a brief outline of the number of doctors who visited Biko].

Should Mr. Biko's death be the result of suicide it would fit into a pattern which has become common among detainees in South Africa. In recent years there have been a large number of deaths by suicide in South Africa among detainees . . .

However, numerous detainees, who have been detained following communist training and indoctrination, have testified that they receive specific instructions to commit suicide rather than divulge information to the police. The result is that in the past 18 months seven detainees have died as a result of hanging and three others have jumped from the windows of high buildings. Police say it is virtually impossible to stop a man determined to commit suicide from doing so and, in any event, the suicides are sometimes totally unexpected.

To their critics the police point out that so far a court of law has never established that the police have been responsible for torturing or killing a single detainee, although all cases are thoroughly investigated. For any reasonable person confronted with this type of anti-South Africa propaganda the question must arise: where South Africa is spending millions and moving mountains to improve her image would she wilfully and purposefully allow something like this to happen to destroy all the good work that has been done? The answer must be: No.

Biko the greatest man I have ever known — *Donald Woods*

In a newspaper article[19] editor Donald Woods wrote:

My most valued friend, Steve Biko, has died in detention. He needs no tributes from me. He never did. He was a special and extraordinary man who at the age of 30 had already acquired a towering status in the hearts and minds of countless thousands of young blacks throughout the length and breadth of South Africa.

In the three years that I grew to know him my conviction never wavered that this was the most important political leader in the entire country, and quite simply the greatest man I have ever had the privilege to know.

Wisdom, humour, compassion, understanding, brilliancy of intellect, unselfishness, modesty, courage—he had all these attributes. You could take the most complex problem to him and he would in one or two sentences strike unerringly to the core of the matter and provide the obvious solution . . .

I once went to Mr. J. T. Kruger and begged him to lift the restrictions on Steve and to speak to him. The result of that visit was an increase in Steve's restrictions and a state prosecution against me.

He always came out of such ordeals [detention] as tough as ever and as resiliently humorous about the interrogation sessions. He had a far closer understanding of his interrogators' fears and motivations than they will ever know, and with almost total recall he recounted to me the full range of their questions. Many were simply incredible . . .

The government quite clearly never understood the extent to which Steve Biko was a man of peace. He was militant in standing up for his principles, yes, but his abiding goal was a peaceful reconciliation of all South Africans, and in this I happen to know he was a moderating influence.

Addressing a meeting of more than 1,000 people, held to mark the death in detention of Mr. Biko, Mr. Donald Woods told of an arrangement he had with Mr. Biko who was aware of the ever-present risk of detention and the possibility that he might die there.

'If any of four reasons for his death was alleged, I would know it was untrue'. One of the four reasons was death through a hunger strike.[20]

No assault — no cover-up — *Kruger*

The Minister of Justice, Mr. Kruger, said in an interview with Mr. John Burns published in the *New York Times* yesterday that the preliminary report on Mr. Steve Biko's death did not give the impression that a police assault was the cause of death.

'I personally do not believe this', he stated, 'I don't believe that my police have done anything wrong . . . If there is anything wrong in the Biko case, I will be surprised . . .

'There will be no cover-up in the Biko case', Mr. Kruger said.[21]

V

The Funeral

Thirteen Western nations sent diplomats to the funeral on 25 September.

Police actions prevented thousands of mourners from reaching the funeral from Johannesburg, Durban, Cape Town and other areas. The police prevented bus convoys from leaving the three main cities on the grounds that they lacked permits; while roadblocks nearer King William's Town turned back hundreds of cars and many buses, as South African police in camouflage uniforms and security policemen were stationed on all major roads leading into the town on 24 and 25 September.

The roadblocks were manned by police armed with FN rifles and machine guns. Thousands of mourners from all over the country were converging on the town for the funeral of Steve Biko. People from the Transvaal had to pass through seven roadblocks. Cars were searched, and many people turned back. Thousands of mourners from the Transvaal were barred from attending the funeral when permits were refused for buses. One of the speakers, Dr. Nthato Motlana, who flew from Johannesburg after he was blocked off when attempting to travel by road, said at the funeral that he had watched as black policemen hauled mourners off the buses in Soweto and assaulted them with truncheons. The physician said he had treated 30 of the mourners, some for fractured skulls, and said he had witnesses who would testify that a number of young women were raped.

Steve Biko was buried in a muddy plot beside the railroad tracks after a marathon funeral that was as much a protest rally against the white minority government's racial policies as a commemoration of the country's foremost young black leader. Several thousand black mourners punched the air with clenched fists and shouted 'Power!' as Biko's coffin was lowered into the grave.

The crowd of more than ten thousand heard speaker after speaker warn the government that Biko's death had pushed blacks further towards violence in their quest for racial equality.

'Please, please, for God's sake listen to us while there is still just a possibility of reasonably peaceful exchange', said the Rt. Revd. Desmond Tutu, Anglican Bishop of Lesotho, leading a group of black churchmen[22].

The post-mortem had been done almost immediately, although the pathologist engaged by the Biko family was only informed after the autopsy had begun. This was completed by 18 September and preliminary reports began to appear in the press concerning findings of brain damage, a finding supported by the appearance of Biko's head at the funeral parlour, where observers noted an injury to the forehead.

Mrs. Ntsiki Biko, the widow of Steve Biko, works as a nursing sister in a mission hospital. After the autopsy had been performed, she spoke about her husband:

Steve Biko was a good man, he was a good father, but above all he was a leader.

His death in detention did not come unexpected to me. I knew that because he was a man of such convictions and beliefs only death could stop him from what he believed in.

But I am not satisfied with the way in which the State has said he died.

The first time she heard of her husband's death was when she was notified by her sister:

No policemen informed me, nobody told me, and it was only through my sister-in-law and my sister that the news reached me.

I was numb with shock. But I kept telling myself, and will continue to tell myself, that my husband died in a struggle, during a struggle for the liberation of the black man in South Africa.

Mrs. Biko spoke of her two sons, the two-year-old who still ran to the phone to call out 'Steve, Steve'; and Nkosinathi who is six and found it hard to accept the death of his father. "I couldn't even bring myself to tell him that Steve was in detention again because he knew something was seriously wrong and said to me, 'no Mama, you must not lie. I know he is dead'."[23]

The Black Consciousness movement was dealt a legal death-blow in October, a month after Biko's death, when there was a massive government crack-down on the remaining opponents of apartheid race policies.

In one sweeping action the government banned the Black People's Convention, SASO, the Black Women's Federation, writers', youth and student organisations and welfare groups in various parts of the country. The bans included some organisations, such as the Christian Institute of Southern Africa, that were not related to the Black Consciousness movement. With six other whites, Dr. Beyers Naude, director of the Christian Institute, was declared a banned person and served with an order restricting his movements and activities for the next five years, confining him to Johannesburg and preventing him from being quoted. (The Christian Institute was an inter-denominational, multi-racial group of clergy and laymen which had strenuously opposed the government's racial policies as being 'unchristian and inhuman'.) Donald Woods, editor and friend of Biko, was also banned, removing him from editorship of the *Daily Dispatch*, where he had been calling for an inquiry into Biko's death.

The World, the daily newspaper published for blacks (although white-owned) was closed down; its editor Percy Qoboza and journalist members of his staff taken into detention. 'They dragged him away as if he had killed somebody', said Qoboza's secretary. 'I'll never forget it . . . it was too much'.[24] The Union of Black Journalists was among the newly-banned organisations.

'I sincerely believe in freedom of the press', commented Minister Kruger, 'but there are people in South Africa who can't write a straight story—they are politically committed'.[25]

Peaceful intentions and protestations of non-violence had not saved them. The Black Consciousness leaders, like those of other once-legal organisations in the past, were now jailed (more than 200 were arrested as the organisations were banned), or silenced and confined. Or, like Steve Biko and Abram Tiro, dead.

Thus the movement that sought to build up among blacks an awareness and pride in their identity, as well as to build black unity, became one with all the others whose real crime was opposition to apartheid. These are the dusty answers to those who ask for freedom.

VI

The Inquest

The inquest was postponed until 14 November. At the end of October, two weeks before it was due to start, announcements were made by both the Attorney-General for the Eastern Cape and the Attorney-General for the Transvaal, that no criminal proceedings would be instituted in the Steve Biko affair.

Two months after his death the inquest on Steve Biko began on 14 November in the Old Synagogue, Pretoria. The Old Synagogue has been the scene of many political trials from the end of the 1950's onwards. It is peculiarly unsuited for any 'public hearing'.

High, large, ornate, the interior was designed without any regard to audience or sound and with little regard to the hot and airless Pretoria climate. The acoustics are appalling; voices become a muffled murmur barely audible except to those placed close to the speakers. The clearest sound disperses and is lost. A huge crowd of spectators and pressmen squeezed into the courtroom every day to listen anxiously, with the added difficulty that most of the evidence was given in Afrikaans. November is summer in South Africa. Outside the streets were lined with jacaranda trees in the full glory of their pale purple blossoms. Inside, the Old Synagogue was described as a 'sauna bath'; its old-fashioned electric fans were switched off in an attempt to improve the sound.

An inquest is held when someone dies from other than natural causes. It is not a trial. There are no 'accused' and no 'defence'. It is in the nature of a public inquiry, presided over by a magistrate; its purpose is to establish the truth of how death came about. The state appoints a prosecutor (in this case Mr. K. von Lieres, Deputy Attorney-General) not to prosecute, but to lead all the available evidence; and also appoints a presiding magistrate (Mr. Marthinus Prins). Two 'assessors' were also appointed—medical experts to assist the magistrate in weighing the medical technicalities.

The police and doctors who were presenting evidence on Biko's death were represented by counsel, as was Biko's family. Counsel were there to advise those concerned on their legal rights, and had the right to question anyone giving evidence.

In a normal inquest, it is sufficient to record the basic facts given in evidence, and the findings of the presiding magistrate at the end. This, however, was no ordinary inquest. It was in essence—as will be shown later—a conspiracy to defeat the ends of justice; a conspiracy in which almost all the witnesses and most of the court officials joined. Their purpose was not to establish the cause of death but to conceal it; not to discover who might be responsible, but to hide them.

For this reason, to present a straight, verbatim account of the proceedings would be to portray the events as the conspirators portrayed them, concealing the truth. To obtain the truth it is necessary for the prosecutor to assemble the evidence in a manner which would clarify events, and in logical sequences. This was not done. It is necessary, too, that witnesses testify precisely. In this case, witnesses appeared together with affidavits made by them at various times before the inquest, often contradictory, partial and obscure. And finally it is necessary that all the 'official' personages in the drama co-operate to let the truth come out. This was not the way in which this inquest was conducted; in contradiction to the theory, counsel for the state, for the police, and for the doctors—all state appointees—ranged themselves together as 'defenders' of their clients against an unspoken, but nevertheless palpable, accusation of complicity.

Sir David Napley, Past President of the British Law Society, who was invited to attend the inquest by the Association of Law Societies of South Africa as an independent observer, expressed some concern over the role of the Deputy Attorney-General in the inquest:

It appeared to me, both on a true reading of the Inquests Act and the decision in the case of Timol, that it was his duty dispassionately to present to, and test, on behalf of the magistrate, all the relevant available evidence.

I may be wrong but I came away with the clear impression that, on such occasions as he intervened, his questions were directed to preserve the position previously taken up. To this end on occasions he intervened to support the police and doctors, although they were already represented by other counsel.

Whilst I am not satisfied that this presence in fact made any significant difference to the outcome of the inquiry, it seemed odd to me that the Deputy Attorney General, having been seen to be asking questions apparently designed to sustain the earlier formed view, should later be called upon to play the decisive part in determining whether criminal proceedings should nevertheless be taken.

Thus, while the summary of events set out here has been abbreviated to make clearer what was alleged to have happened on each of the vital days from the time of Biko's arrest until his death, it must be borne in mind that even this simple outline—even the barest bones of the Biko story, distilled to its leanest from the evidence—may not be wholly correct.

The account of the inquest that follows has been pieced together from the very full reports published every day in the *Rand Daily Mail*. Some of the evidence is given in the form of direct speech and some indirect, as it was reported. It was not possible (for reasons of time) to obtain the full court transcript, have it translated from Afrikaans (in which most of the evidence was given) and give the evidence of each witness in his original words, but the substance is here.

The inquest was high drama. Never before at an inquest of someone who died in detention have there been television cameras and reporters from so many countries. Even in the USA the press, usually closed to such events in South Africa, published daily reports. The Johannesburg *Sunday Times* had a vivid description of the television crews, camped in the yard with sunshades and cool bags, while every day a crowd of black spectators sang outside the Synagogue.[26]

Inside, four members of the Biko family sat on a bench against a side wall while a young, bearded white man sat with them acting as interpreter. In a few days nearly the entire foreign press corps was on the floor at his feet, listening too.

Bit by bit the information about Biko's last days began to emerge. But more than that. Day after day South Africa revealed itself through the evidence and the men who gave it. The inquest of Steve Biko was not simply an exceptional event; it was, in a sense, a revelation of racism, of the way it has distorted ordinary people, and the way it has destroyed all morality and decency in a rich and beautiful country.

Personnel at the Inquest

State Prosecutor	Mr. K. von Lieres
Presiding Magistrate	Mr. Marthinus Prins, assisted by Professor I. Gordon of the Natal University Medical School, and Professor J. Oliver of the University of the Orange Free State Medical School
Counsel for the Biko Family	Mr. Sydney Kentridge, assisted by Mr. E. Wentzel and Mr. G. Bizos
Counsel for the Police	Mr. Retief van Rooyen, assisted by Mr. J. M. C. Smit
Counsel for the Doctors	Mr. B. de V. Pickard, assisted by Dr. Marquard de Villiers.
Police Witnesses	Colonel Pieter Goosen, Chief of the Security Police in the Eastern Cape Major Harold Snyman, leader of the day interrogation team of whom the four other members were: Captain D. P. Siebert Warrant Officer Marx Warrant Officer Beneke Detective Sergeant Nieuwoudt Lieut. E. Wilken (security police) Warrant Officer Fouche Sgt. P. J. Van Vuuren
Doctors	Dr. Ivor Lang, district surgeon Dr. B. J. Tucker, chief district surgeon Dr. C. Hersch, consultant Dr. van Zyl, district surgeon, Pretoria

Pathologists	Dr. Loubser, state pathologist
	Dr. Gluckman, for Biko family
	Professor I. Simpson
	Professor Proctor
Police Investigating Officer	Gen. Kleinhaus

Sequence of events, 18 August to 12 September

18 August Biko is arrested.

Steve Biko was travelling in a car with a friend Peter Jones, an executive member of the BPC. The car was stopped outside the King William's Town limits at a roadblock, by Lieut. Oosthuizen of the Security Police. The two men were taken to Grahamstown; the next day they were taken to Walmer Jail, Port Elizabeth and held under Section 6 of the Terrorism Act, in the custody of the Security Police under the command of Colonel Goosen.

He is kept naked in a cell for 20 days. Port Elizabeth.

For the next twenty days Biko was kept at Walmer Police Station, naked, manacled, and not allowed out of his cell even for air or exercise. His daily ration of food was soup, magewu,* bread, jam and coffee.

According to the sergeant in command, the soup and magewu were refused, and Biko ate little bread.

2 September, Magistrate's visit.

On 1 September a magistrate made a formal visit to Biko in his cell. Biko complained that he had not even been permitted to wash himself. He asked the magistrate for water and soap to wash himself and a washcloth and comb.

He asked: "Is it compulsory that I have to be naked? I have been naked since I came here".

The magistrate made no reply.

6 September, Biko taken for interrogation to Room 619 Sanlam Building in Port Elizabeth.

On the morning of 6 September, Biko was taken from the Walmer Street prison by security police, and brought to Room 619, Sanlam Building, for interrogation. The police state that they were with him from 10.30 a.m. until 6 p.m. From 6 p.m. he was in the care of the 'night squad' (led by Lt. Wilken) naked, handcuffed and with one leg chained to a grille.

Room 619 at 7 a.m. on 7 September.

Major Harold Snyman, head of the interrogation team of five, arrived at 7 a.m. and according to his statement, removed Biko's leg-irons and handcuffs. At this time, or very close to it, Biko received the blows that caused brain

---

* magewu — sour maize drink.

31

damage and resulted in his death five days later. The police were unable to continue their interrogation. Biko was again handcuffed and chained to the grille.

7.30 a.m. on 7 September, Biko already has brain injury.

Colonel Goosen was informed that there had been an "incident". At 7.30 he arrived at Room 619 and spoke to Biko, who, he said, seemed incoherent and talked in a slurred manner. There was a visible swelling on his upper lip.

9.30 a.m. Dr. Lang gives medical check-up.

The district surgeon, Dr. Lang, was called in. He examined Biko in the presence of Col. Goosen. At the Colonel's request he made out a certificate that there was no evidence of any abnormality nor pathology on Biko.

Night of 7 September. Biko lies on mat, chained and in leg-irons.

The Security Police attempted once more to interrogate Biko, but he was totally unresponsive. For the rest of that day, and for that night, Biko lay on a mat on the office floor, manacled and chained by his leg as before.

8 September, Dr. Lang comes and brings Dr. Tucker.

Dr. Lang returned. Col. Goosen told him that Biko had not urinated during the past 24 hours, and had refused all offers of food. Lang re-examined Biko, and then requested that the chief district surgeon, Dr. B. J. Tucker, examine Biko with him.

Although the trousers Biko had been wearing (for the interrogation) and the blankets were now soaked with urine, Dr. Lang noticed no change and Dr. Tucker did not question Biko. It was decided to transfer him to the prison hospital.

Evening of 8 September, Biko is taken to prison hospital.

A specialist physician, Dr. Hersch, was consulted; it was agreed that a lumbar puncture should be performed. Biko was transferred to the prison hospital.

Night of 8 September, Prison hospital.

A warder stated that during the night of 8 September he twice found Biko lying in a bath, the first time clothed in a bath filled with water; the second time the bath was empty.

9 September.

The lumbar puncture was performed early in the morning.

10 September.

Hersch informed Lang that the lumbar puncture showed the cerebro-spinal fluid to be bloodstained. It was decided to consult a neuro-surgeon, Mr. Keeley, by telephone; Keeley gave the opinion that there was no evidence of brain damage, but Biko should be kept under observation.

He saw no reason why Biko should not be transferred back from hospital to the Security Police, provided he was kept under observation.

11 September
Biko is taken
back to a cell.

In the morning the Security Police took Biko from the hospital, and bed, back to a cell at Walmer Police Station. He was left on a mat on the cement floor of the cell, naked under the blankets.

He is found
collapsed.

A few hours later a warder found Biko lying on the floor with foam at his mouth, and glassy-eyed. He informed Major Fischer, who phoned Col. Goosen.

He is driven
naked through the
night to Pretoria.

Dr. Tucker examined Biko at 3.20 p.m. and saw no objection to Goosen sending Biko on a journey of 740 miles by road to Pretoria. Naked and manacled, he was left lying on the floor of a Land-Rover, with nothing except a container of water.

11—12 September,
Pretoria Prison.

He was carried into the prison hospital and left on the floor of a cell, without any medical records, 11 hours after leaving Port Elizabeth.

12 September
Dr. van Zyl gives
intravenous drip.

Several hours later, a newly-qualified doctor, with no medical information about him other than that he was refusing to eat, ordered an intravenous drip.

Biko dies.

Some time that night Biko died, unattended.

VII

The Police

The Arrest

Affidavit: Lieutenant Alfred Oosthuizen, of Grahamstown Police.

On 18 August Oosthuizen received information that inflammatory pamphlets were being distributed inciting blacks to cause riots.

He learnt that Biko was on his way between King William's Town and Cape Town, and had reason to suspect he was actively concerned in the distribution of the inflammatory pamphlets.

At 8 p.m. he put up a roadblock, and at 10.20 a white station wagon was stopped.

The driver and his passenger were both cheeky and made derogatory remarks. When the passenger was told to get out of the vehicle he asked, in a belittling manner, if that was normal procedure—then he got out.

The driver identified himself as Peter Jones, and the passenger as Bantu Biko. They would not give further details. Oosthuizen decided to take them to the charge office.

There he asked Biko if he had permission to be outside King William's Town district to which he was confined. Biko said he had no written permission, and he could do as he liked.

Biko laughed at him, and in doing so fell on a bench, which broke.

Lieut. Oosthuizen tried to search Biko and Jones, but they refused to allow him to, and Biko grabbed his hands. Finally he did search them.

Biko wanted to take his private possessions with him to the cell, but was told this was not permitted.

Oosthuizen then got in touch with his commanding officer, who told him to take the two men to Port Elizabeth. This was done the next day.

*　　*　　*

The evidence appears to be straightforward, yet there are several matters which are not explained:

If Biko was outside King William's Town, he was clearly in breach of the banning order confining him there, and subject to criminal charge. Why was he never charged?

If there was 'reason to suspect' Biko's participation in the distribution of inflammatory pamphlets, why was he asked only about his right to leave King William's Town?

34

As no leaflets were found in the car, why was Biko detained at all at this time? If there was a prior intention to detain him under Section 6, he could have been picked up at any time at his home in King William's Town. What, therefore, was the purpose of setting up a roadblock?

In Walmer Police Station

For the next twenty days (from 18 August to 6 September) Biko was held in a cell at Walmer Police Station, Port Elizabeth. He was held incommunicado and in solitary confinement, unable to contact anyone in the outside world and denied communication with others inside the jail. He was without books, papers, materials of any kind. He was not allowed any exercise and he was naked.

Witness: Sgt. Paul Janse van Vuuren, Warder

Kentridge	Why naked?
Van Vuuren	On the instructions of Colonel Goosen, head of Security Police in Port Elizabeth.
Kentridge	Was Biko kept naked to humiliate him?
Van Vuuren	I cannot say. From 18 August to 6 September Biko was not allowed out of his cell.
Kentridge	Isn't a prisoner entitled to exercise in the open air?
Van Vuuren	I was acting on instructions from Colonel Goosen.

Witness: Major Snyman

Kentridge	Why naked?
Snyman	On instructions given to prevent a recurrence of suicide in police cells.
Kentridge	Are you suggesting a man can commit suicide with a pair of underpants? You still let him have blankets. People have committed suicide with their blankets.

Witness: Colonel Goosen

Goosen	There was a clear pattern of suicide among detainees during the past few years; everything with which detainees could hurt themselves, including the clothes of male detainees, were taken away.
Kentridge	The warrant under which Biko had been arrested made provision for personal clothing to be kept available for him.
Goosen	There had been incidents where detainees had used their clothes to commit suicide.
Kentridge	Is there any reason why a man for decency's sake should not be allowed to wear a pair of underpants?
Goosen	It was to prevent suicide.

Kentridge	Have you ever come across a case of suicide with strips of blankets ?
Goosen	Not in 23 years.
Kentridge	Had you given orders that Biko be kept naked when transferred to the Port Elizabeth prison on September 8 ?
Goosen	I cannot remember that I gave that order.
Kentridge	Weren't you afraid that while in prison he may commit suicide ?
Goosen	He was in a prison hospital with staff who would nurse him.

Witness: Sgt. van Vuuren

He had visited Biko daily from 18 August to 6 September. Biko never complained. His impression was that Biko did not want to speak.

He gave Biko meals of soup, magewu, bread, margarine, jam and coffee.

Biko refused the soup and magewu, and the bread heaped up. He did not ask for any other food.

Affidavit from visiting magistrate*

He saw Biko at the Walmer police cells on 2 September; Biko asked for water and soap to wash himself, and a washcloth and comb.

Biko said: 'I want to be allowed to buy food. I live on bread only here. Is it compulsory that I have to be naked? I have been naked since I came here'

Witness: Colonel Goosen

Kentridge	During the time Biko had been in Walmer police cells he had not been allowed any exercise on your instructions ?
Goosen	I am being wrongly interpreted. Biko had been alone in a cell and had enough fresh air and could get enough exercise. He had not been allowed out of the cell.
Kentridge	According to prison regulations, prisoners who do no outdoor work should be allowed one hour's exercise in the open air whenever the weather permitted. What right did you have to override a standing instruction ?

Interjection from P. R. Van Rooyen, (Counsel for the Police):

The questions have nothing to do with the cause of death but are part of a 'vendetta' against the security police.

The inquest should not be used as a platform for propaganda against the security police. Its only purpose is to investigate if anybody could be blamed for Mr. Biko's death.

---

*The Terrorism Act allows for a magistrate to visit a detainee where this is possible. Previous detention acts also provided for magistrates' visits. There is no single instant in which any complaint made to a magistrate is known to have been taken any further. Everything said to the magistrate is handed over to the security police.

Goosen   Sections of the Press and liberalists have created a climate of revolt against security legislation among the general public.

There is a lot of agitation and criticism against the security police.

It has developed so far that South Africans are getting guilt feelings that we might have acted incorrectly. Therefore the security police are very careful not to give any reasons for criticism.

We are very disappointed by this criticism because we are aware of the politeness and concern with which we treat detainees. We buy them cigarettes, cold drinks and nice things to eat.

Assault charges would harm the image of the security police.

Under cross-examination from van Rooyen, Goosen enlarged on the care taken to see detainees were not injured. 'We have no reason to assault a detainee', he said, and added: 'No assault charges have ever been laid against my assaulting team'. Laughter followed and he changed the phrase to 'the interrogation team'.

Goosen   Because there was a tendency to suicide in police cells, like the Baader-Meinhof cases in Germany, we do our utmost to prevent this. If a detainee complains of only so much as a headache, a doctor is called.

If a prisoner suffers, for instance, from high blood pressure, it is arranged that he should be regularly visited by a doctor.

Biko's health had been of the greatest importance. Because of information in my possession I realised that it was of primary importance to bring this 'peaceable' man before a court.

Witness: Lieutenant Gert Kuhn, second in command at Walmer Police Station.

He had visited Biko in the course of his duties. He had never received complaints from him. He had not been told by other policemen that Biko would not eat, or had complained.

He did see him lying under a blanket without clothes.

There was always fresh water in the cell, but because Biko never complained he had not checked to see if the water was being drunk. He had seen no injuries on Biko, and in particular had not seen the bruise on the left side of his forehead which appeared on a photograph handed to him.

Lieut. Kuhn had made three statements on these events, he said. In the first he gave a list of times when he visited Biko in his cell, including the dates 8, 9 and 10 September which were after the date on which Biko 'became unwell'. He had seen no injuries on Biko, he said, and had no knowledge of any incident in which Biko could have been injured.

In his third statement, however, Kuhn gave another list of dates on which he had visited Biko's cell, omitting 8, 9 and 10 September. He said his first state-ment was not false—'just faulty'. It was rectified in a later statement.

He inserted the times into the affidavit without checking them. He knew his evidence would be used to show that on those dates there was nothing wrong with Biko.

He had not seen Biko after 6 September.

He realised the dates in his affidavit were incorrect only when his attention was drawn to this by Mr. von Lieres at a consultation.

*   *   *

The question as to why Biko was kept naked during his whole detention—except during interrogation when he was permitted to wear a shirt and trousers—is dealt with more fully both by the British law observer, Sir David Napley, and in comment at the end of the inquest.

Kentridge's question about suicide with strips of blankets referred to the death in September 1976 of Luke Mazwembe who the police claimed had cut a blanket into strips and hanged himself within two hours of being arrested.

The 'pattern of suicide' among detainees does not stand up to scrutiny.

Lieut. Kuhn's 'faulty' statement is in line with many other statements that were contradictory, faulty, or simply false.

Sanlam Buildings — 6 September

Witness: Major Harold Snyman, Security Police

He was the leader of an investigation team of five appointed to interrogate 'the Black Power detainees'.

Biko had been detained on 19 August, but for strategic purposes others were interrogated first. On 6 September it was decided that Biko should be confronted with certain evidence. He was taken to office 619 in the Sanlam Building in Port Elizabeth, which besides being the offices of one of South Africa's largest insurance companies also houses the Port Elizabeth Security Police H.Q. Earlier, Snyman had testified that Biko had been permitted to wear trousers and a short-sleeved shirt during interrogation.

The interrogation began at 10.30 a.m. and lasted till 6 p.m.

Biko adopted an extremely aggressive attitude. To make him feel at ease, his handcuffs were removed and he was offered a chair to sit on.

He was offered meat pies and milk, which he refused. It was strange, that he did not use the toilet.

Biko evaded questions concerning his activities. He would not answer any questions directly: but as the interrogation went on he was more co-operative.

Among other things, he said that he had gone to Cape Town to escape his marital problems.

Later he said his sole purpose in going was to heal a breach which had arisen in the Black People's Convention.

Biko admitted he and Patrick Titi, another detainee, were responsible for compiling the pamphlets distributed in Port Elizabeth on 17 August.

Kentridge   What method of persuasion did you use to make an unwilling witness talk to you? That morning Biko denied all knowledge of a certain pamphlet, and by 6 p.m. he had admitted drawing it up?

Snyman   Biko was confronted with certain evidence the security police had, then he admitted it.

Kentridge   He first denied it and then admitted it? Why should he answer you at all? Why shouldn't he just whistle at you? Did you make threats?

Snyman   No.

Kentridge   Did you put physical pressure on him?

Snyman   No.

Kentridge   How did you break him down?

Snyman   We told Biko he would remain in detention until he had answered the questions satisfactorily.

Kentridge   Biko was detained in 1976 for 101 days. What sort of a threat do you think it would be to him to threaten to keep him in detention unless he answered questions? What can you do to a man who insists on keeping silent?

No answer.

Mr. Kentridge repeated the question several times.

Kentridge   You are evading my questions. At the beginning he gave a denial. Later on he gave proper information. How do you get him from the first stage to the second stage?

Interruption by Mr. R. van Rooyen.

Major Snyman had already replied that Biko admitted his involvement after being confronted with evidence gleaned from other sources.

Snyman   After I went off duty at 6 p.m. on 6 September, Biko was allowed to rest until 7 a.m. the next day. I decided not to send him back to the Walmer Police Station because of his importance and his aggressive attitude.

Kentridge   That is nonsense. He could have been taken back in the same way he was brought to the Sanlam Building—in handcuffs and in a police car—to the comparative comfort of the cell where he would not have had to sleep in chains.

Snyman   We have had problems with information at police cells.

Kentridge   You were afraid that information could leak out through your own personnel?

Snyman   Yes, through cleaners and people taking in food. It was learnt in the past that 'leftists' came to the police cells and communicated with detainees.

Kentridge	What was it that you did not want to leak out? Were you not afraid that what would leak out was the way in which he was treated? *No answer.*
Kentridge	Major Snyman, at that time, how many detainees were there at your headquarters?
Snyman	Only Biko.
Kentridge	And at 6 p.m., after your first day of interrogation, you were relieved by Lieutenant Wilken's night squad of three?
Snyman	Correct.
Kentridge	They were the night interrogators, were they?
Snyman	Correct.
Kentridge	Did you report to Lt. Wilken how far your interrogation of Biko had progressed?
Snyman	It wasn't necessary, as they were only there to guard him while he rested.
Kentridge	Oh come, come, are you saying that those three men simply came in to watch Biko?
Snyman	Correct.
Kentridge	Oh come, Major Snyman, you know that that must be nonsense. Isn't it obvious that these three men were there for the purpose of night interrogation?
Snyman	Certainly not.
Kentridge	Then why did you agree with me a few minutes ago that they were the night interrogators?
Snyman	No, I didn't agree with you.

The court record was then re-read, and the court agreed that Snyman had in fact stated that the men were night interrogators.

Kentridge	Although you have the right, of course, to have the questions interpreted into Afrikaans, did you understand my use of the English word 'interrogators'?
Snyman	I understand the word.

Witness: Colonel Pieter Johannes Goosen, Divisional Commander, Eastern Province Security Police.

On 6 September Biko was being questioned in Room No. 619 in Sanlam Buildings by the team under the command of Major Snyman. Major Snyman reported to him that Biko did not eat or drink.

He visited Biko, but could not see anything physically wrong with him. It appeared Biko had also not used toilet facilities.

He was not worried because Biko was very big and strongly built and he attributed his reluctance to eat food to his obstinacy over answering questions.

Arrangements were made that the questioning take place from 7 a.m. to 6 p.m. with adequate rest periods in-between.

After 6 p.m. a team under the command of Lieutenant Wilken had to come on duty to look after him continually during the night. The necessary sleeping mats with blankets were given to Mr. Biko.

The night of 6 September

Witness: Lieutenant Winston Eric Wilken

He made a point of visiting Biko from time to time during the night of 6 September.

He believed he was alone when he spoke to Biko in Room 619 and that Biko was asleep most of the night.

Kentridge	Did you seriously believe a man could sleep through the night with leg irons and handcuffs ?
Wilken	A person generally woke up in the night in any event even if they did not have on leg irons and handcuffs. Biko had only one foot in the leg iron which gave him a lot of mobility. When I said Biko was asleep, I meant that his eyes were not open. Biko was loosely manacled and the pressure of the leg iron would not always be felt as a weight on the leg. The pressure would be the same as that on a person who was wearing sunglasses—he would be aware of them.

He agreed that Biko's one foot and ankle were swollen.

Kentridge	According to medical evidence to be introduced, it appears probable that Biko suffered head injuries either during the night of 6 September or in the early morning of 7 September before 7.30 a.m. If that is the case, the responsibility would appear to lie with your night squad or Major Snyman's day squad.
Wilken	I cannot throw any light on how Mr. Biko might have suffered an injury while under my care, or how an injury could have occurred on 6 September.

Witness: Warrant Officer Henry Fouche

His instructions had been to guard Mr. Biko who was handcuffed and chained to an iron grille with a leg iron.

Kentridge	Did you stay in the room with him ?
Fouche	We were in the general office most of the time.
Kentridge	Did Lieut. Wilken stay in the room with Biko for any length of time ?
Fouche	Not that I can remember.

Kentridge	What would you say if I suggested that he sat on a chair and spent several minutes looking at Biko?
Fouche	It is possible.
Kentridge	Why should he do such a thing?
Fouche	To pass the time.
Kentridge	If you are in the general office, can you hear talking from Room 619?
Fouche	Yes, unless they whispered.
Kentridge	Are you an interrogator?
Fouche	No.
Kentridge	During the night of the 7th do you remember that Lieut. Wilken spoke to Biko?
Fouche	Correct.
Kentridge	What did he speak to him about?
Fouche	I heard voices coming from 619 and I went there and heard Lieut. Wilken offering Biko food. Biko indicated that he didn't want it and turned around.
Kentridge	Did you hear Lieut. Wilken say anything else to Biko?
Fouche	No. I didn't hear what was being said. After a few minutes Lieut. Wilken came out.
Kentridge	Did Lieut. Wilken seem pleased with himself?
Fouche	He is always good-humoured. He looked the same as usual. He told me nothing. He did not say if Biko had made a statement.
Kentridge	When next did one of you go into Biko's room?
Fouche	Within half an hour Lieut. Wilken again went to Room 619 and he stayed there for perhaps a minute.
Kentridge	Did you hear at any time from Lieut. Wilken that Biko had agreed to make a statement?
Fouche	No.

Witness: Lieut. Wilken

When he made his second statement, dated 20 October, he had been informed that Gen. Kleinhaus was investigating the circumstances which led to Biko's death. He was shown a photograph where an external mark above the left eye was pointed out.

'It was put to me that it was possible Biko received this injury while he was under my control. I was warned by Gen. Kleinhaus that I was not obliged to make any further statement.

'When the photo of Biko's face was shown to me with the mark above the left eye, I now remember that when I arrived on duty on the evening of 6 September, just after 6 p.m., while Biko was lying on his back with his face to the ceiling, I saw a darkening of the skin similar to a birthmark, dark brown, above his left eye and more or less on the same position as that on the photo. I placed no value on it. It did not look like an injury to me. Biko made no complaints to me'.

42

Kentridge	When you took over on 6 September you were there to continue the interrogation?
Wilken	No.
Kentridge	Does it not seem strange that a lieutenant and two warrant officers should be detailed to stand watch over a man chained hand and foot?
Wilken	Yes, probably under normal circumstances. That was the Colonel's instructions.
Kentridge	Major Snyman agreed with me that you were on the night interrogating team with your two assistants.
Wilken	That is not so.
Kentridge	What did Biko mean when he said, give me 15 minutes?
Wilken	Biko said give me 15 minutes.
Kentridge	You must have been pretty pleased that he was prepared to give you a statement?
Wilken	I was surprised and pleased.
Kentridge	That was very good for a non-interrogator.
Wilken	Yes.
Kentridge	Did you then get a sheet of paper and a pen?
Wilken	It was too early for pen and paper; we would have first got a verbal story.
Kentridge	Did you go back after 15 minutes?
Wilken	Yes, he was asleep.
Kentridge	Why did you not wake him up?
Wilken	It was . . . (*inaudible*) not my instructions to wake him up.
Kentridge	You made a big break-through—you said you were quite pleased.
Wilken	My instructions were to leave him and let him rest; and when it seemed he was asleep I left him.
Kentridge	Did you not think it strange that he said 15 minutes and then you find him asleep?
Wilken	He may have taken me for a ride.
Kentridge	Then about an hour later he woke up?
Wilken	Right.

Kentridge drew the Court's attention to the fact that Lieut. Wilken was the only one of a number of officers who saw Biko during his detention in Port Elizabeth who had noticed the mark on his forehead.

Wilken said he had noticed the mark—which appeared to be a birthmark—above Biko's left eye while he was sitting in a chair next to Biko's bed.

Kentridge	What were you doing sitting next to Biko?
Wilken	I just wanted to sit there. I was killing time.
Kentridge	I know there has been an attempt to create the impression that you were just night nurses, but weren't you sitting on the chair to ask a few questions?

Wilken	The light was on, and I was looking at Biko. Later that night I returned to pass a few more minutes.
Kentridge	On the second occasion you actually went to sit on the chair to look at Biko in the dark?
Wilken	Laughable as it may sound, that is so. It was not so dark that I could not see Biko.
Kentridge	I ask you to take the court into your confidence. What were you really doing in that office that evening?
Wilken	I don't know if that is an insinuation, but nothing happened. Biko was never assaulted while under my care.

*   *   *

It seems unlikely that Wilken and his two colleagues were simply there to guard Biko while he slept; a shackled man scarcely needs three guards.

The usual method of security police interrogation is constant, uninterrupted questioning, often continued over several nights and days. Testimony of this by numerous detainees over many years is incontrovertible.

Sanlam Building — 8 September

At 7 a.m. the next morning the day interrogation team came on duty and relieved Lieut. Wilken and the two warrant officers. The day team consisted of Major Snyman, Capt. Siebert, Warrant Officer Beneke, Det. Sgt. Nieuwoudt and Warrant Officer Marx, although the last two claimed to have been in an adjoining room when the other re-commenced the interrogation.

All five of these police officers gave an account of a 'scuffle' or struggle which took place between them and Biko shortly after 7 a.m.

Witness: Captain Siebert

Before they continued their interrogation the next morning he and Major Snyman (the leader of the interrogation team) discussed their tactics. They realised that the easy-going method of question and answer was not getting them far and they decided to use the more aggressive method of confronting him with the facts. This had succeeded the previous afternoon. Biko had cracked.

He was present throughout the struggle that took place that day.

Biko had fallen twice—the first time in the area of the chair in which he had been sitting and the second time face down near the bed.

It was not impossible that he had bumped his head against the wall.

Kentridge	Did you see him fall with his head against the wall?
Siebert	No.

44

Witness: Major Harold Snyman

Shortly after 7 a.m. Biko had his leg-irons and handcuffs removed, and was offered a chair to sit on; he got a wild expression in his eyes suddenly, and jumped off the chair.

Biko threw the chair at him, but he jumped out of the way.

After this, Biko charged at Warrant Officer J. Beneke, lashed out wildly at him, and pinned him against a steel cabinet.

Witness and Captain Siebert went to W/O Beneke's help. They tried to grab Biko who was clearly beside himself with fury. In the process they knocked against tables in the office.

Two other members of the team came to assist. They over-powered Biko, then put handcuffs and leg-irons on him.

The struggle lasted several minutes. He could not say how long exactly. It took place in a limited space and they bumped against tables and the walls.

Biko still did not calm down. He was fastened to the grille in the office but continued to struggle against his handcuffs and leg-irons.

At 7.30 that morning he reported the incident to Colonel Goosen. They both visited Biko in office 619.

Colonel Goosen spoke to Biko, who still had a wild expression in his eyes. 'I noticed there was a visible swelling on his upper lip'. He was talking incoherently and in a slurred manner.

Biko refused to react to questions and the wild expression remained in his eyes. At 9.30 the district surgeon, Dr. Lang, gave him a medical check-up. Witness was not present. Later he and the team tried to communicate with Biko, but he would not react to questions.

He then gave orders that Biko was to be allowed to rest on his mat and covered with a blanket. He was still handcuffed and the leg-irons were fixed to the grille.

He was offered water repeatedly but mumbled refusal.

Biko was passed into the custody of the night team under Lieutenant Wilken.

Kentridge	At no time before the morning of the 7th did Biko show any sign of violence. What need was there to put him in leg-irons on the 6th?
Snyman	The office was not locked.
Kentridge	Could you not have locked it? I think you will have to give a better answer. Why did you put him in leg-irons? Was it to break the man down, or only to prevent escape?
Snyman	It was the custom.
Van Rooyen	You were there; why did he go berserk?
Snyman	I confronted him with certain facts. He jumped up immediately like a man possessed. I ascribe that to the revelations that I made to him.
Van Rooyen	What would you say if it was put to you that you pulled these 'facts' out of thin air?

45

Snyman	We had the facts.
Van Rooyen	... The sworn statements about the authorship of the pamphlets? The typing of it? The roneoing of it? And the offices where it happened? About the real purpose of his visit to Cape Town and planning of the united front?

Mr. Van Rooyen then asked to hand in the pamphlets, and sworn statements by other detainees, as evidence. Mr. Kentridge said he understood that the sworn statements put to Biko were part of the reason for his sudden wild outburst. These sworn statements were put to Biko on the 6th or on the morning of the 7th? Snyman replied: on the morning of the 7th.

Kentridge then checked with the magistrate that the date of the affidavits ranged from 15 September to 30 September.

Kentridge	These could not have been put to him during his lifetime. What we have got here is a smear prepared after Biko's death and I think it is a disgrace.
Van Rooyen	It was the contents of the documents that had been put to Biko.
Kentridge	It was made quite clear that the sworn affidavits were put to Biko. That is why I confirmed myself that they were actually put to Biko. I called on the witness to put it beyond doubt.

The magistrate ruled that the sworn statements would not be permitted as evidence.

Witness: Captain Siebert

During the interrrogation Biko said at one stage: 'You are intimidating me'. Then they put it to him that he fell in the category of urban terrorist.

The interrogators did not call Biko an urban terrorist to his face. They implied it by the facts they mentioned.

Biko was shocked. He was 'ashen grey'. Then he said 'You are intimidating me, you are harassing me'. He had said this during the interrogation and again repeatedly during the struggle.

Kentridge	Biko is not merely being tried. He is being convicted. It was their aim to discredit Biko in his life-time. Not having succeeded, they are trying to do it now.
Siebert	At one stage during the violent struggle Biko fell flat with his face on the floor. There was no other incident in my presence when Biko could have hurt himself. He was never hit at or slapped at by anybody in my presence.
	Immediately after the incident, Major Snyman reported it to Col. Goosen who came into the interrogation room and tried to communicate with Biko.
	Biko was still beside himself with fury and spoke in a slurred manner.
	Goosen then left the interrogation room.

	Because of his mental condition, no further communication was possible with him and the interrogation was interrupted. At 9.30 a.m. the district surgeon examined Biko. The interrogation team then tried again to communicate with him, without success.
	Biko had never had the appearance of having been 'smashed up'.
Kentridge	The story about Mr. Biko falling flat on his face is not contained in your statement to Major-General Kleinhaus, the investigating officer?
Siebert	I said in my statement it was not impossible Biko had sustained his injury while the police were trying to restrain him.
Kentridge	Why didn't you tell Gen. Kleinhaus? You knew he was interested in finding out how the injuries could have been incurred.
	No answer.
Kentridge	There is no answer to that question is there?

Witness: Warrant Officer Ruben Marx, Security Police

On 7 September at 7 a.m., he went on duty with the rest of the team, but was working on other matters in the room alongside the interrogation room.

At about 7.20 a.m. as a result of a hard bang, he and Detective-Sergeant Nieuwoudt charged into the interrogation room. When he went into the office he saw Major Snyman, Captain Siebert, and Warrant Officer Beneke struggling with Biko. 'He was raving in fury'. He and Sergeant Nieuwoudt rushed to the help of their colleagues. For a few minutes they managed to hold him down to the floor. 'We fastened his hands and feet to the grille'. (Later amended to feet only).

During the struggle Biko jumped up and screamed: 'You are harassing and you are intimidating me'.

Kentridge	This morning Major Snyman used those same words. Eleven statements have been previously made about what happened in that room on the morning of the 7th. In not one of these statements is there anything about Biko shouting out; and now this morning for the first time we have the exact same words from you and from Major Snyman. I put it to you that this is an invention.
Marx	It is not a fabrication.
Kentridge	In the Occurrence Book on 8 September Major Snyman reported Biko fell with his head against a wall and his body on the ground, and in the process suffered an injury to his lip and his body. Is that true?
Marx	I know of an injury to his upper lip.
Kentridge	I am asking you whether the statement by Major Snyman is true or not.
Marx	I didn't see him hit his head against the wall.
Kentridge	Did you see him fall on his head?
Marx	No.

Kentridge	Were you interested in what caused the death?
Marx	I guessed, I am not a doctor . . . possibly as a result of the skirmish we had. That was a possibility. There was a heavy struggle.
Kentridge	As a result of the skirmish you had? What gave you that idea?
Marx	In that skirmish any reasonable person can believe that he may have got an injury.
Kentridge	Really? Did you tell that to General Kleinhaus?
Marx	Questions were put to me and I answered them.
Kentridge	Did you put this theory of yours to General Kleinhaus?
Marx	I answered his questions and he didn't ask me to elaborate.

*　　*　　*

Whatever the nature of the assault on Biko the results were such that Col. Goosen was immediately summoned.

Witness: Colonel Goosen

About 7.30 a.m. Major Snyman reported that Biko had become very aggressive and had thrown a chair at him and had attacked W/O Beneke with his fists.

He immediately visited Biko in office No. 619. He found him sitting on the mat with his hands handcuffed and the leg-irons shackled to an iron bar grille.

He noticed a swelling on Biko's upper lip. No other injuries or bruises could be noticed. His eyes affected a wild expression.

Biko was very aggressive and had pulled and pushed on the handcuffs.

He immediately tried to phone the district surgeon, Dr. Lang. He was told Dr. Lang was doing his prison rounds.

He left messages for Dr. Lang to phone him urgently.

Dr. Lang arrived at his offices about 9.30 a.m. Witness was present at the examination. Except for his swollen upper lip, Biko had no other external injuries. After the investigation Dr. Lang gave him a certificate which read:

'This is to certify that I have examined Steve Biko as a result of a request from Col. Goosen of the Security Police, who complained that the above-mentioned would not speak.

I have found no evidence of any abnormality or pathology on the detainee.'

This was signed by Dr. Lang at 10.10 a.m. on 7 September.

Kentridge	Is it true—that he 'would not speak'—or false?
Goosen	I have already said we had difficulty in communicating. I may have used the term mentioned. I said we had problems with communication and that includes 'would not speak'. I wanted to have Biko medically examined to make sure he had not been assaulted.
Kentridge	Yes. Then why did you say in your (later) affidavit you were worried he had had a stroke?

Goosen replied that he could see no other injuries beside one on his upper lip and because of his extremely tense state he feared Biko had possibly had a stroke.

This was a purely logical inference. Biko had behaved like a wild animal and there was something wrong with his speech.

He had mentioned to Dr. Lang that he thought Biko might have had a stroke.

Kentridge Why did you request a medical certificate from Dr. Lang?

Goosen It was a logical step. I knew there would be tremendous propaganda if anything would happen to him.

Kentridge The reason is you were worried that afterwards he would say he had been assaulted. You wanted a certificate to show he had not been.

Goosen I don't think this was the reason.

Witness: Major Harold Snyman

He stated that he made an entry in the Occurrence Book on 8 September because Biko stubbornly refused to answer questions and he felt he was 'shamming'.

He did not say in the Occurrence Book that Biko was 'shamming' but only mentioned the struggle and possible injuries.

He thought Biko was shamming because he had no external injuries and 'never asked for a tablet or anything'. He did not look ill.

Kentridge The entry in the Occurrence Book reads: 'The detainee was very aggressive, then became berserk, threw a chair at me, and rushed with clenched fists at other members of the staff. After a tremendous struggle he fell with his head against a wall and sustained an injury on his body'.

Snyman During the struggle Biko fell several times against walls, cabinets and the bars.

He had reported to Colonel Goosen that Biko had suffered a blow on the head when he fell against the wall.

Witness: Col. Goosen

Kentridge Do you know why this entry in the occurrence book was not made on 7 September after the incident?

Goosen I would suggest that the entry had not been made on the 7th because there was a medical certificate to say there was nothing physically wrong with Biko; but on 8 September an entry had been made because there had been further concern about Biko which made it necessary.

Kentridge Had Major Snyman told you what he had written in the occurrence book?

Goosen In broad outline.

Kentridge Did he tell you at any time that during the scuffle in room 619 on 7 September Biko had fallen with his head against the wall?

Goosen	I don't believe that the term 'head against the wall' was specifically used. He said there was a heavy struggle.
Kentridge	Did any of the officers say that Biko had bumped his head in any way?
Goosen	Not in so many words. I made the deduction that it was probable he might have.
Kentridge	You have made five affidavits in this case. In your affidavit on 21 October you deal specifically with the way you thought Biko could have had the injury to his forehead. This is the one you made when Gen. Kleinhaus told you he died as a result of brain injury and he showed you the photo of the mark above Biko's eye. And yet neither in this affidavit nor in any other do you make the suggestion that he might have had a bump on his head in the struggle in the office.
Goosen	I thought of it as a possibility.
Kentridge	The possibility was mentioned nowhere in the affidavit?
Goosen	It didn't allow for possibility.

Witness: Captain Siebert

Prins (*magistrate*)	When you took Mr. Biko for a medical examination on 8 September you said Biko could walk normally without assistance. I have a statement from Warrant Officer Beneke which said Biko had to be supported by black warders when he left the prison van.
Siebert	This support had not been the support one would give to an unconscious man. [*He took hold of the interpreter's elbow to demonstrate*]. Two black warders had held Biko by the arm to safeguard him and prevent his escaping.

He had not seen the mark on Biko's left forehead.

Kentridge had remarked on the fact that both Snyman and Marx had used identical words when describing the 'scuffle' with Biko. Siebert was to have followed on, but von Lieres made an attempt to change the order of the witnesses. Kentridge's objection to this was upheld; but when von Lieres had to call Siebert, he did not ask him to give his version of what took place.

*   *   *

The incident of the Occurrence Book is one of the most interesting and revealing. Where a prisoner is kept under restraint, such as in chains as in Biko's case, standing orders provide for this to be noted in an Occurrence Book, kept at the police stations. As Kentridge mentioned later, this is not left to police discretion, but is mandatory. The Security Police, as always above the law, did not keep such a book in Sanlam Building. Goosen later claimed it was left to his discretion.

No entries were made concerning Biko prior to 8 September, when Snyman went to the police station to make an entry 'because he felt Biko was shamming'

—an entirely illogical reason for the late entry. When Goosen says no entry was made on the 7th 'because there was a medical certificate to say that there was nothing physically wrong with Biko', he was for once speaking the truth: he had possession of the medical certificate. But the medical certificate itself was false. By the next day, when Biko's deteriorating condition gave cause for alarm, an attempt was made to record a 'scuffle' in which he might have sustained his injuries.

While some comment is needed regarding the 'scuffle', this is not a simple matter. Did the scuffle ever take place? If it did, why were the police unable to explain adequately how Biko received an injury to his forehead during the scuffle?

From the evidence, particularly that later given by medical experts, it emerges that if any 'scuffle' did take place, it occurred *after* Biko had received the injury to his brain.

In a book called *Injuries of the Brain and Spinal Cord and their Coverings* by Sir Charles Symonds, there is a description of someone who has sustained a brain injury. After a period of unconsciousness he would be 'unaware of his environment and be inaccessible . . . He is at first mute, unresponsive to commands and inert . . . Later he begins to be restless and while still mute and stuperous may become restive and violent'.

Napley also remarks that Biko's so-called violence was not the reaction of a normal man. 'What was he to gain by it? No one suggested anything. If it was unrestrained anger no evidence suggested that his temperament normally manifested that trait'.

The five men involved in the scuffle were brought into court. They were all big, well-developed and strong men. The whole idea that they had difficulty in controlling Biko seemed absurd.

Why, then, is there no acceptable account of some accidental knock on Biko's forehead? They could have said he fell, knocking his head against a table. Why the difficulty in concocting some evidence of this kind?

In fact, as emerged in evidence that was given later by the medical experts, there were vital pieces of medical evidence that the police could not have known the experts would be able to establish with such certainty. These concerned the nature of the injury, the timing of it, and what would have happened immediately after it was inflicted, and show clearly that the probable time Biko was injured was early on the morning of 7 September, while he was in the custody of either Wilken's night squad or Snyman's day squad.

There was in court a concerted attempt by all witnesses to deflect attention away from Wilken's team, by presenting them not as interrogators but simply as those who guarded Biko while he slept. Yet it is most improbable that Wilken's team did not question Biko during the night. That is doubtless what they were there for—and why else the curious account of how, at one point in the night, Biko asked for 15 minutes, apparently in order to give a statement, and, after that interval, according to Wilken, appeared to be asleep. This *could* be a garbled account of the undeniable period of unconsciousness.

From the evidence presented the fatal blows could have taken place either just before or just after Snyman's team took over from the night interrogators. At first sight Snyman's team appears the most likely to have assaulted Biko, if only because under questioning, its members recalled a 'scuffle' in which Biko might have been injured—though none witnessed it happening. The 'scuffle' however, may have taken place when Biko recovered consciousness, and jerked about uncontrollably. His 'wild behaviour' would thus have been the result of blows received somewhat earlier, in Wilken's custody. Sir David Napley certainly found Wilken the most 'vicious and terrifying' of all the police witnesses:

Lt. Wilken, on entering the court, presented an air of amiability to all concerned, and spent some time smiling. At one point, when his face was turned from the Magistrate and he became put out by a reference by Mr. Kentridge to his having played the part of a night nurse, he revealed, when taken off his guard, a picture, to which his eyes gave testimony, of underlying anger and a degree of viciousness which I personally found to be terrifying.

It is possible, therefore, that the fatal blows were struck by Wilken and his team, leaving Snyman to cope with the results and to call in his superior, Goosen, when their gravity became apparent. Apart from obtaining the certificate from Dr. Lang, however, nothing more was done until the following day.

* * *

On the morning of 8th, Biko's condition must have caused some anxiety because Goosen ordered another medical examination.

Witness: Colonel Goosen

Goosen	I told Dr. Tucker and Dr. Lang of my suspicions because Biko had not taken food or liquid. We had here a man who would not eat, react or talk and who used no toilet facilities. I still thought he was shamming. I had had experience before with this tendency.
Kentridge	Do you think it shamming if a man does not go to a toilet for three days ?
Goosen	I knew there had been a violent struggle but did not know for certain what injuries could have been incurred.
Kentridge	Why did you not mention this to the doctors ? You told the doctors you were worried about a stroke but never that you were worried about a head injury. My submission will be that you knew Biko might have suffered a head injury but wanted to draw the doctors' attention away from it.
Goosen	That is not so.
Kentridge	When the doctors arrived Biko was still shackled hand and foot. After they had left he was again shackled. In terms of a standing order it had to be noted in an occurrence book if a prisoner was put under restraint in this way ?

52

Goosen	Security police officers do not keep occurrence books.
Kentridge	I don't understand your answer. Are you saying you are above standing orders in the Security Branch?
Goosen	Standing orders are guidelines.
Kentridge	To be obeyed or not as you might see fit?
Goosen	My security officers have no occurrence book and I have never had an order to keep one.
Kentridge	From the time of the morning of the 7th, excluding the time of interrogation and the examination by the doctors, Biko remained in chains. What right did you have to keep a man in chains for 48 hours?
Goosen	I have the full power to do it. Prisoners could attempt suicide or escape.
Kentridge	Let's have an honest answer—where did you get your powers?
Goosen	It is my power.
Kentridge	Are you people above the law?
Goosen	I have full powers to ensure a man's safety.
Kentridge	I am asking for the statute.
Goosen	We don't work under statutes.
Kentridge	Thank you very much. That is what we have always suspected.

Goosen said he had not meant he was above the statutes, but that he was using his own sound judgement.

Kentridge	The standing order makes provision that when a person is kept under this sort of restraint an entry has to be made in an occurrence book, and there is no room for discretion?
Goosen	At a normal police station there would be no discretion.
Kentridge	It doesn't apply to you?
Goosen	Where there is no occurrence book it would be left to my discretion.
Kentridge	Why did you not go to a police station where there is an occurrence book?
Goosen	Then I would have to do it every time.
Kentridge	Yes, quite right—every time you put a man in chains.
Goosen	I would have been running backwards and forwards to the police station all the time.
Kentridge	I want to know what sort of man you are. Would you keep a dog chained in this way for 48 hours?
Goosen	If a dog is an absolute danger I would probably do it. Here in this case this was the position.
Kentridge	He was so dangerous that he had to lie on his mat in chains for 48 hours?
Goosen	I had to protect him.

53

Kentridge	You certainly succeeded. He never got out of your hands . . . he was let out to die.
Goosen	He was not. Everything possible was done to keep him alive.

*   *   *

Doctors Lang and Tucker suggested that Biko should be examined by a specialist physician, and for this purpose he was transferred to a prison hospital where there would be 'better facilities for a proper examination'. The transfer took place after dark on the evening of the 8th.

Witness: Colonel Goosen

Kentridge	Col. Bothma said that you gave instructions that Biko should be guarded only by white members of the police force. Did you not trust the black members of the force?
Goosen	This was one of my standing instructions in all these cases of detention. Black policemen were not always available. The prison hospital was manned by whites and this order had been given to prevent any messages being passed.
Kentridge	Doesn't this and the fact that Biko was taken to the prison only after dark seem as if you didn't want anybody to know that Biko suffered from an ailment?
Goosen	Quarters used for awaiting trial prisoners had to be cleared for Biko. I had to consult with Col. Bothma and I was told that the doctor could see Biko only late that night.

Witness: Warrant Officer Jacobus Beneke

Kentridge	That evening you helped to take Biko to the prison hospital?
Beneke	Correct.
Kentridge	How did you help to put him to bed?
Beneke	I just stood by and drew the blankets away from him. Biko was dressed when he was taken to hospital. He was wearing the trousers he had been wearing all the time while in custody.
Kentridge	What was the state of these trousers?
Beneke	There was nothing wrong.
Kentridge	What was the state of his mat and blankets?
Beneke	The mats were just as they had been. The blankets were a bit disarranged.
Kentridge	The doctors found that he had urinated while in that bed?
Beneke	Every time I went in he was under the blankets.
Kentridge	His trousers and blankets were never changed?
Beneke	No.

Sydenham Prison Hospital, Port Elizabeth — 9 September

According to evidence given by a policeman, he found Biko out of his hospital bed twice during the night and morning of 8/9 September. The first time was 3 a.m., when he found Biko sitting in a bath of water with his clothes on. A few hours later he was again found in the bath, but the second time it was empty.

Witness: Warder J. Fitchet (detailed to guard Biko on the day of 9 September).

Cross-examined by E. Wentzel, acting with Kentridge for the Biko family.

Fitchet   On 9 September Biko stated he wanted to exercise, got out of the bed and walked around his cell for about 20 minutes. He walked without any aid and without holding on to anything. He did not appear unsteady on his feet. He kept his head down with his eyes fastened to the ground. After about 20 minutes he said he was tired and sat on his bed.

Wentzel   I am told that in the light of his medical condition it is inconceivable that on 9 September he could have walked round in the manner you describe. What would you say about that?

Fitchet held on to the microphone in the dock and remained silent.

Wentzel   You won't get inspiration from the microphone.
Fitchet   I cannot answer that question.

Some time later, Fitchet added he had been asked by Gen. Kleinhaus, police investigator, to fill out a duplicated statement in connection with Biko's detention. The person filling it in had to cross out incorrect statements and add further comments if he felt it necessary.

Wentzel   A large number of affidavits in this form have been sworn to as evidence in this inquest. In this form you were asked to cross out what did not apply and to leave in what did apply. You have crossed out the following words:
    'Besides what I already said in my statement(s) I noticed no injuries of any kind on Steven Biko'.

Fitchet also crossed out the statement: 'I noticed the following injury(s) on Steve Biko during my visit to him'.

The following statement remains standing in the roneoed form: 'I noticed no injury of any kind on Steven Biko'. Fitchet added the words . . . 'except handcuff marks on both wrists'.

The other statement left standing on the form was the following: 'I was shown a mark on a photo taken during a post-mortem on Steve Biko. I have not noticed such a mark or injury on Steven Biko'.

Wentzel   Did Gen. Kleinhaus give you instructions whether to cross out what didn't apply while you were alone, or with other warders?
Fitchet   He gave us no instructions.

Wentzel	Did he give you an explanation that you were to do the roneoed forms when you were alone, or when your colleagues were with you?
Fitchet	I am not sure.
Wentzel	It is less than a month ago. Do you have a particularly bad memory?
Fitchet	Yes.

Witness: Colonel Goosen

Kentridge	In your statement you deal at length with the fact that Biko was found on the morning of 9 September in a bath and later on the floor next to the bed. You put forward, as a probability at least, a theory that that is why he suffered his brain injury. Why didn't you put forward, as a possibility, your theory that it might have happened in the course of the struggle on the morning of the 7th?
Goosen	He was found in the bath full of water. I thought there might have been an attempt at suicide.
Kentridge	There are two possibilities. Why did you only mention one? I'm going to tell you why. It is because you were putting up a theory which took it as far as possible away from your own men.

*   *   *

A lumbar puncture was performed on Biko on the morning of the 9th. Biko remained in the prison hospital that day and night (there is no evidence of his condition.)

On 10 September, the specialist, Dr. Hersch, informed Dr. Lang (who first visited Biko on the 7th) that the lumbar puncture showed the cerebro-spinal fluid to be blood-stained. A neuro-surgeon, Dr. Keeley, was consulted by phone, but did not object to Biko being transferred back to the security police.

On the morning of the 11th, Biko was taken back to a mat at the Walmer Police Station.

*   *   *

No explanation was given as to how Biko, who the police had stated had to be manacled and chained for fear he might try to escape, was left apparently unguarded in the prison hospital, and was able to fill a bath with water and climb into it before being discovered.

It could be that the two incidents actually took place (but as with other police evidence, there is no reason to assume this to be true) in which case it would have been symptomatic of the disorientation arising out of the brain damage. Or it could have been an invention to try and explain how Biko sustained his brain damage.

56

Walmer Jail — 11 September

Early on Sunday 11 September Biko was transferred from the prison hospital (where he had apparently received no treatment of any kind, apart from the lumbar puncture for the purposes of diagnosis) and was taken back to a cell at Walmer Police Station. There he was in the charge of Sgt. van Vuuren, who had been in charge of him during his detention prior to his being taken to Sanlam Buildings.

Witness: Sergeant Paul Janse van Vuuren

On 11 September he saw that Biko had been returned. That evening he visited Cell No. 5, where Biko was kept.

To get into the cell one had to go through four locked doors.

Biko seemed to be asleep on his mats. Later he found him on the cement floor with his head towards the cell bars and his feet near the mats.

He could not say if Biko had fallen or crawled to that position.

Biko was found lying on his right side looking at the door. There was froth on his mouth and his eyes were glazed.

He tried to give Biko water, but he stayed in the same position.

He took hold of Biko under his arms from behind ('like a lifesaver' commented Magistrate Prins), dragged him onto the mats, covered him with blankets and called the Security Police.

He saw no injuries on Biko, in particular not the bruise on Mr. Biko's forehead appearing in the photograph shown to him.

At 6.20 p.m. on 11 September he booked Biko out of the Walmer Police Station. He did not know where he was taken.

Witness: Colonel Goosen

About 2 p.m. on 11 September he was phoned by Maj. Fischer and visited Biko in his cell.

Biko was lying on his mat and his breathing was somewhat irregular. A little foam was on his lips. He immediately phoned Dr. Tucker.

At 3.20 Dr. Tucker examined Biko. Both doctors expressed concern because the nature of any possible upset could not be diagnosed. It was agreed to transfer Biko to an institution with all possible facilities.

He phoned Brigadier Zietsman of the Security Police headquarters in Pretoria. He received instructions to transfer Biko to the Central Prison in Pretoria. If no military plane was available, road transport was to be used if the senior district surgeon had no objections.

No planes were available and Dr. Tucker had no objections to road transport to Pretoria for Biko if he was provided with a mattress or something soft to lie on.

Everything possible was done by him to see to the comforts and health of Biko while he was in detention.

Goosen ordered that Biko should be sent to Pretoria because they had the facilities for a proper examination there.

Kentridge	What was wrong with Port Elizabeth? There are very good hospitals in Port Elizabeth.
Goosen	I still thought he was feigning. I thought it was possible that he could be assisted to escape and leave the country. I have often had prisoners under guard in hospitals who succeeded in escaping.
Kentridge	Wasn't the real reason that you did not want anybody to see Biko in that condition? You did not think he would die and until he recovered you wanted to keep him out of sight.
Goosen	I had no reason to hide him. Neither I nor any of my colleagues nor the doctors saw any external injuries. When I could not get a military plane I asked Dr. Tucker if I could convey Biko by road. Dr. Tucker said that provided they allowed Biko to lie on a soft mattress there was no reason why not.
Kentridge	What facilities was Biko to have?
Goosen	A relatively luxurious Land-Rover was used. Seats were removed to put the mattress on the floor.
Kentridge	We understand that the only facility available was a container of water?
Goosen	We still thought he was shamming. The doctors did not prescribe anything.
Kentridge	The prison regulations say that in cases of death, serious illness and injury, the prison department has to notify the next of kin of the prisoner. Biko's illness had been serious enough to warrant examination by a specialist and to send him 700 miles to a hospital in Pretoria. Why didn't you notify his next of kin?
Goosen	After the doctors had examined him it was their opinion that there was nothing physically wrong. I had no reason to inform his family. I had reason to believe he was shamming. Biko was sent to Pretoria for diagnosis.
Kentridge	You thought there was nothing wrong, yet on the Sunday night you tried to get a military plane to take this malingerer to Pretoria?
Goosen	This shows the attention we gave him. Even when a prisoner has only a headache he gets a doctor. I tried to get Mr Biko to Pretoria as soon as possible.
Kentridge	Do you know that Dr. Hersch took a lumbar puncture and that the finding was positive? Red blood cells were found in the spinal fluid.
Goosen	To my knowledge the three doctors said they could find nothing wrong.
Kentridge	If all these doctors told you there was nothing wrong, why did you try to get a military plane?

58

Goosen	This showed the care we took to avoid criticism.
Kentridge	I put it to you that the dictates of common humanity and decency would have impelled you to inform the family unless you had something to hide.
Goosen	The circumstances were special. We were trying to prove that Biko was somebody quite different from what he had seemed to be. Had we known he was ill the family would have been told.

The Ride to Pretoria—Night of 11 - 12 September

The men who accompanied the now dying Biko on the night ride from Port Elizabeth were three members of the interrogation team, Capt. Siebert, Lieut. Wilken and W/O Nieuwoudt.

Witness: Captain D. P. Siebert, Security Police, Port Elizabeth

Biko was taken naked to Pretoria. He thought that being naked might place a damper on any escape attempt. He was still not sure if Biko was shamming an illness or not.

Kentridge	Did consideration of common humanity bear no weight with you?
Siebert	Yes, I am humane.

Lieutenant Wilken and Warrant Officer Nieuwoudt travelled in the back of the Land-Rover with Biko.

Kentridge	What medical equipment did they take with them in the back of the van?
Siebert	They only had a container with water.

Biko was covered with blankets.

They had left Port Elizabeth at 6.30 in the evening and had arrived in Pretoria the next morning. They stopped on the road to take in fuel at a couple of police stations, but Biko never left the van.

He had sat in the front of the vehicle and had inquired from time to time if Biko was sleeping. He was told that he was but sometimes when lights were shone into the vehicle at police stations he saw that Biko was awake.

Kentridge	Was he breathing normally?
Siebert	When we approached the vehicle to unload him and he saw us approaching he started breathing deeply.

When Biko was taken into the Pretoria prison his condition had not changed. He still thought Biko was shamming. He could not say that he was worried.

Kentridge	Sergeant Pretorius, medical orderly at Pretoria, has given a statement that on the morning of his death Biko had looked seriously ill and he was afraid for his life. One of the security men had told him that Biko had studied medicine for four years, that he practised yoga and could mislead other people.

59

Siebert	Biko had been examined by doctors in Port Elizabeth and they considered his condition to be such that he could be taken to Pretoria by car. I understood that to mean that the possibility that Biko was shamming was not excluded.
Kentridge	I can understand people saying to doctors and others: 'It is difficult to say what happened to him, we don't know if he is shamming, but you had better know that he had had a bump on the head'. When Sgt. Pretorius said he thought the man was sick, all you gave was the theory of shamming.
Siebert	I can't even remember if I talked to Pretorius personally. One of my colleagues could have talked to him or he could have overheard us.

Witness: Lieut. Winston Eric Wilken

On the trip to Pretoria, he travelled in the back of the Land Rover. Before the trip commenced he and Detective-Sergeant Nieuwoudt had tried to put on Biko's clothes, but he had resisted. They had put him on a mat and carried him to the Land Rover.

They had no co-operation from him, but he had no reason to think Biko was sick. He was not a doctor and could not say whether the man was in a state of collapse.

Kentridge	Did you notice that the man was in a state of semi-coma?
Wilken	He did not give me that impression.
Prof. Gordon	Why did you think a man was being taken 740 miles to Pretoria if he was just shamming?
Wilken	I was told he was going to Pretoria for observation. I knew he was not going for specific treatment.
Kentridge	Why was this a night journey?
Wilken	I didn't make the decision and I didn't ask anybody. I never questioned the decision. He might have had to be in Pretoria early in the morning.
Kentridge	Wasn't it very unusual to take a detainee to Pretoria in this manner?
Wilken	No.

Biko apparently slept most of the way. When they stopped for petrol he did not give Biko a chance to get out to stretch his legs. He was given an opportunity to relieve himself, but he did not want to do so. He could not remember when the offer was made to Biko.

Kentridge	During the journey was Biko in any state to talk to you?
Wilken	I can't remember that he talked to us except to refuse water and other facilities. He was offered water but I cannot remember that he took any.
Kentridge	Fit as a fiddle was he?
Wilken	He was all right.

Kentridge	I am suggesting that this cannot be true. You must have seen that you had a very ill man on your hands?
Wilken	He was awake.
Kentridge	Did you help to carry him into the Pretoria Prison?
Wilken	I was present but did not carry him. I don't know why he didn't walk. He was offered a stretcher.
Kentridge	But the telex* stated that he took water on two occasions.
Wilken	I can remember that Sgt. Nieuwoudt offered him water on two occasions.

When they arrived in Pretoria Biko's condition was the same, normal.

Kentridge	He was normal, and now we are speaking of some 12 hours before his death?
Wilken	That is correct.
Kentridge	Do you remember one of your party saying to the other that Biko had studied medicine for four years, that he practised yoga and that he could deceive people easily?
Wilken	It is quite possible that I had said it myself because at that stage I believed Biko was shamming. While we were in the Land Rover Biko would breathe normally, but when there were lights and people around he would breathe more deeply. His breathing at particular times only made it appear that he had been shamming.
Kentridge	What right did you have to say this man could deceive people and was probably shamming?
Wilken	It was an opinion.
Kentridge	Why is it you security people insist on telling people all the time that he was shamming?
Wilken	The case was that the doctors had said there was nothing wrong. We had to assume they were right.
Kentridge	Is not the obvious reason that there was something you wanted to hide in connection with this man?
Wilken	No, we had nothing to fear or hide.
Kentridge	You are sent on an urgent journey to Pretoria on a Sunday night, to take a man to hospital. He had, according to you, refused food and water, nor taken any opportunity in the course of a 12 to 14-hour journey to relieve himself. He said, as far as we know, not a word during the journey. And then when you get to Pretoria you take it upon yourself to tell people in Pretoria that this is a person who can easily deceive others and you think he is shamming. Is that a reasonable summary of what happened?
Wilken	It is one-sided if you don't take in the background; but basically, yes, it's correct.

---

*From Goosen to Security HQ (*see below*).

| Kentridge | I suggest that it was not Biko that was shamming but members of the security police. I am going to suggest that this constant refrain was to draw attention away from what the security police had actually done. |
| | *Reply inaudible.* |

Pretoria Prison — 12 September

Some hours after arriving in Pretoria, Biko was examined by a local district surgeon, who told the Court he had been practising medicine for two years.

Witness: Dr. Andries Van Zyl, Pretoria District Surgeon

He had examined Biko at the Pretoria Prison Hospital at 3 p.m. on 12 September.

Before 12 September, he had never been in the section where Biko was kept.

He had been told Biko had refused to 'partake of anything' for a week. Also that Biko had been examined by a doctor and a physician who could not find 'any fault' with him.

He received no record from Port Elizabeth in connection with the patient. After examining Biko he diagnosed general weakness and dehydration as a result of his having had 'no food or liquid' for seven days.

He prescribed a drip, and gave Biko a vitamin injection.

Kentridge	Who gave you the history of Biko's alleged refusal to eat or drink for seven days?
Van Zyl	I learnt this in a telephone conversation with a Sgt. Pretorius at the Central Prison hospital. As far as I remember no one told me Biko's case was urgent.
Kentridge	Did Mr. Biko seem seriously ill?
Van Zyl	He was medically a sick, sick person . . . he was comatose.
Kentridge	Where did you hear that the Port Elizabeth doctors could find nothing wrong with Biko?
Van Zyl	One of the warders told me that.

He added that he did not know who the warder was, and he was not introduced to him. He had not been told at any stage that doctors had found signs of neurological damage on Biko.

He had tried unsuccessfully to talk to Biko, but could get no reaction. He was with Biko 30 to 45 minutes, possibly longer.

Von Lieres	Was the room in which Biko was kept equipped satisfactorily?
Van Zyl	He had been taken to different wards, which looked like those in a hospital. Biko was in a private room.
Kentridge	On these photographs of the room, it looks as though the patient was lying on a mat on the floor, and not on a bed.

Van Zyl	It appears to be the correct place.
Kentridge	When you saw Biko, was he on mats on the floor?
Van Zyl	That is correct.

*   *   *

The existence of a telex message sent by Col. Goosen to Security Police Headquarters in Pretoria was revealed in the closing days of the inquest. Goosen in evidence had denied its existence; but it was revealed by Brigadier Zietsman, Head of the Security Police in Pretoria.

Kentridge sought permission to call the Brigadier as a witness, to probe the investigation carried out by the Brigadier after Biko's death. But this the magistrate refused.

Commenting on this, Sir David Napley, observing on behalf of the Law Society, wrote:

> I had the impression that when the magistrate (as I believe, by misdirecting himself on the law) refused permission for Brigadier Zietsman to be called as a witness, he had not appreciated that it would remain open to Mr. Kentridge to cross-examine Colonel Goosen as to information contained in the Brigadier's affidavit.

The message was telexed on 16 September—four days after Biko's death—and stated that Biko's injury was 'inflicted' at 7 a.m. on 7 September.

Witness: Colonel Goosen

Kentridge	You told us that no telex had been sent from your office.
Goosen	No telex message directly concerning Biko's injury.
Kentridge	We have been given a telex message by courtesy of Brigadier Zietsman signed by you and dated the 16th.
Goosen	It concerns the transport arrangements.
Kentridge	It also deals with Biko's injury?
Goosen	I'd like to see it.
Kentridge	Why didn't you tell us about it before?
Goosen	It concerned transport arrangements.
Kentridge	When Major-General J. F. Kleinhaus came to investigate didn't he ask for documents?
Goosen	No.
Kentridge	Didn't he search your offices?
Goosen	No.
Kentridge	The telex message addressed by you to security headquarters, Pretoria, refers to a telephonic conversation between you and Col. du Preez dealing with the circumstances and methods of transporting Biko to Pretoria . . . You further said that the matter was urgent because Biko's condition had deteriorated since he was admitted to the cells on the 11th. You said that at the time of his

admission he could still walk, but later gave the impression that he was in a semi-coma.

In your evidence you would never concede that Biko had been in a semi-coma?

Goosen	It was never clearly put to me in Court.
Kentridge	You gave the impression that you did not regard the matter as urgent?
Goosen	I did not regard it as urgent that he should get to an institution where he could be treated.
Kentridge	In the telex message you also say that the district surgeon felt Biko should be removed to a prison where facilities were available. You said he did not eat and that small quantities of water were given to him on two occasions, that at times he was asleep and at times awake. Is that in accordance with your evidence that your impression at the time was that there was nothing seriously wrong?
Goosen	I did say that we were worried about his condition.
Kentridge	You said that the telex had nothing to do with the injuries, yet in it you said he had sustained injuries at 7 a.m. on 7 September; and that these were covered by an entry in the occurrence book; and that after the injury he refused to speak. Were you tying up his refusal to speak with his injuries?
Goosen	A telex is a very short summary.
Kentridge	You refer to the injury 'which was inflicted'. By the 16th you were talking about an injury which had been inflicted on the detainee?
Goosen	It was an inference.
Kentridge	An inference that who had inflicted the injury?
Goosen	That it had been inflicted during the scuffle.

Kentridge then referred to a telephone conversation Goosen had had with Brigadier Zietsman, who asked how far the questioning of Biko had progressed.

Kentridge	You told him that Biko had indicated that he wanted 15 minutes to consider, but after 15 minutes indicated that he no longer wanted to co-operate?
Goosen	Correct. Lieut. Wilken had told me Biko had asked for 15 minutes.
Kentridge	Brigadier Zietsman had asked how far the examination had progressed and that was your answer?
Goosen	Correct. We discussed it only in broad outline.
Kentridge	On the basis of this I suggest that the whole story about Biko having made a confession must have been a fabrication?
Goosen	No.
Kentridge	If Major Snyman had told you what he told the court, that Biko had made a confession, you would have told Brigadier Zietsman that Biko had confessed to sending out pamphlets?
Goosen	I did not discuss the matter in detail with Brig. Zietsman.

64

Kentridge	If you knew about the confession you would have told Brig. Zietsman? He later spoke to you again and asked for questions about Biko's arrest, the time from which he would not eat and his removal to the prison hospital.
Goosen	Correct.
Kentridge	He said at no stage did you say Biko had verbally threatened a hunger strike?
Goosen	I had never said he would go on hunger strike.
Kentridge	You were aware of the statement by the Minister of Police which indicated that Biko had verbally threatened a hunger strike? Can you give any assistance in understanding how the Minister came to make such a statement?
Goosen	I cannot comment at all on Press statements made by the Minister.

VIII

The Pathologists

The cause of death revealed in the medical evidence was not disputed. Death was brought about by complications following on brain injury. Biko suffered at least three brain lesions occasioned by the application of force to his head; the injury was suffered between the night of 6 September and 7.30 a.m. on 7 September.

It also established that such brain injury is always followed by a period of unconsciousness of between 10 minutes and one hour.

The evidence that follows concerns the post-mortem and is given by those who participated. Three pathologists testified to the primary injury sustained in Room 619.

The Post Mortem

Witness: Professor Johan Loubser, Chief State Pathologist in Pretoria

He had performed a post mortem examination of Biko's body on 13 September. There had been no sign of dehydration. Leaving aside secondary haemorrhage, there were five distinct lesions in Mr. Biko's brain. Two of these lesions might have been noticed macroscopically (with the naked eye).

Kentridge	Professor Proctor concluded that the lesions were 'clearly indicative of severe traumatic brain contusions and contusional necrosis'.
Loubser	Agreed. The contusions [bruises] came from a 'mechanical origin'.
Kentridge	The infliction of these lesions would have required at least three, but probably four, blows to the head, usage of the word blow meaning the application of force to the head. The first lesion was what has been called a contracoup, meaning an injury on one side of the brain, caused by a blow on the other side of the head?
Loubser	It is my considered opinion that the main lesion was caused by a blow on the left-hand side of the forehead. I have considered it, and I am of the opinion that the lesions can be explained by a single force applied which hit the left frontal region on such a broad base that the direction of the impulse fanned out.
Kentridge	That would be a very powerful application of force. Could it be due to a fall?

66

Loubser	Yes.
Kentridge	What about a blow from a blunt object such as a rubber truncheon?
Loubser	I would have difficulty in explaining the size of the wound. The scab that appeared on the surface of Mr. Biko's head was the one aspect of the injury that could be compatible with this.
Kentridge	Is there a possibility of two or three blows having caused the injury?
Loubser	This theory seemed consistent only with the exterior of Mr. Biko's skin.
Kentridge	Looking at it externally, this lesion might have been caused by a blow from a fist?
Loubser	I can only agree with such a possibility in the abstract.
Kentridge	What about the fist of a man wearing a ring?
Loubser	That is conceivable.
Kentridge	For the injury to have been caused by a fall, it would have had to be a fall that involved the left side of the forehead, including the cheekbone, but not the nose.
Loubser	Agreed. It would have to be a fall on the left side of the face with the head turned towards the right.
Kentridge	In a normal case of a person falling forward there is an automatic reflex action whereby a person stretches out his hands to save himself. If a fall caused Mr. Biko's injury it would have been a fall allowing his forehead to hit the ground. An epileptic could fall in this way during a fit. Or someone who had been knocked unconscious. What I find difficult to believe was that a conscious man falling to the ground could sustain such an injury.
Loubser	This might be difficult.
Kentridge	If a man fell on his face or forehead there might be some reason to think that he could not use his hands to save himself?
Loubser	Yes.
Kentridge	This kind of injury could be caused by a fall, but it could also be caused if somebody's head were taken and banged against the wall or the floor?
Loubser	It is conceivable.
Kentridge	Referring to your previous evidence that the brain injuries might have been caused by a man bumping his own head against a wall, you are not advancing as a theory that this is what happened, are you?
Loubser	I cannot put it forward as a probability, nor aside as a possibility.
Kentridge	Would that mean that such a man stood in front of a wall and dashed his head against it?
Loubser	Yes, repeatedly.

The Magistrate intervened:

Prins	A person in a struggle could bump his head against a wall and this could have been repeated?
Loubser	Correct. I have not in my experience found a similar lesion as a self-inflicted injury, but there is always a first time.

Mr. Kentridge showed Professor Loubser two photographs, one of a man lying in the position in which Biko had been chained and another of the man in the position Biko might have been if he had been sitting up.

Kentridge	Let us say that Biko had been sitting up with the wall on his right hand side. In order to knock his head against the wall to cause the injury on the left side of his forehead he would have had to contort himself in a rather extraordinary fashion?
Loubser	Correct.
Kentridge	Taking into account the physical contortions necessary, it would seem very unlikely that a man in that position could have inflicted such a wound on himself?
Loubser	If such a person should have lunged forward with his neck turned, it could have been a conceivable way of inflicting such an injury.
Kentridge	That is one possibility in a hundred million?
Loubser	That is possible.
Kentridge	It is a far-fetched possibility?
Loubser	I still consider it an alternative—far-fetched as it might be.
Kentridge	You mean he banged his head repeatedly on the floor?
Loubser	No, I mean he fell over on his left.
Kentridge	I must submit that is really impossible. Assuming that a man shackled to a grille somehow lost his balance and fell then the necessary acceleration could not have been achieved?
Loubser	I don't think he could have fallen. I mean he energetically lunged forward.
Prins	Can you explain what you mean by lunging forward?
Loubser	A fast, strong movement from the legs. He would have had to kick against the wall and with that movement to dive into the floor as a deliberate action. It would have been impossible to knock his head against the wall.
Kentridge	If a man wanted to bang his head he could do it on the wall next to him. Only then it would have been on the wrong side.

Mr. van Rooyen (for the police) intervened here by recalling the police account of 'restraining' Biko.

Van Rooyen	Evidence has been given of an incident on the morning of 7 September when Mr. Biko allegedly went berserk, assaulted people and had to be restrained by force. There has been no evidence that anybody thought that he bumped his head against the wall, but the head moved freely on the neck. If there is a

reasonable possibility that the head connected with the wall in an acceleration movement, if the left forehead bumped against the wall, there would have been a bruising of the type found?

Loubser   Correct.

Van Rooyen   There was no evidence that anybody saw Mr. Biko fall with his left side of his forehead against the floor. But if that happened could that have caused the injury?

Loubser   I don't want to put it as a probability. It could be a possibility.

Witness: Professor Neville Proctor, Professor of Anatomical Pathology, University of Witwatersrand.

He had been practising as a neuropathologist for 25 years and he must have examined several thousand brains.

Prins   Could any one or all of the brain lesions have caused death?

Proctor   The combined effect of all five would have done this. Lesion No. 1 was in itself enough to cause death. Treatment might have prevented Mr. Biko's possible death from oedema.

Kentridge   It is possible to explain all the lesions in terms of a single blow to the left forehead?

Proctor   Everyone agreed that the injury to the left forehead region and lesion No. 1 was contracoup. In my opinion all the lesions were not caused by a single blow and I believe there must have been at least three blows.

Witness: Professor Ian Simpson, Head of Department of Pathology, University of Pretoria.

He was present at Biko's post mortem at the invitation of Prof. Loubser. Since he had submitted the post mortem report he had modified his opinions slightly on some of the lesions found in Mr. Biko's brain.

Pathological evidence indicated that only one application of force, to Biko's left forehead, caused the five lesions in his brain.

He believed the five lesions were of the contracoup type.

       *   *   *

Despite the slight areas of disagreement, all three pathologists were agreed that blows, or a blow, to the head caused Biko's death. The inquiry then moved on to consider the immediate consequences of such an attack.

Witness: Prof. Loubser

Kentridge   Drawing on the authority of Sir Charles Symons, such a degree of brain injury must have been followed by a period of unconsciousness of not less than two minutes, possibly as much as two or three hours. The neurological experts advising us have

69

	expressed the view that Biko's injury must have been followed by a period of unconsciousness of at least 10 minutes, more likely 15 to 20 minutes, and possibly up to one hour. Do you agree?
Loubser	I have no reason to disagree.
Prins	Can you say if a man with that type of injury would recover immediately or whether he would be unconscious for a long time?
Loubser	I would say damage of that region would have led to unconsciousness. I would have expected the injury to have been associated with unconsciousness but would not have been surprised if unconsciousness had not happened. I would have regarded unconsciousness as more than a 50% possibility.
Van Rooyen	You cannot rule out the possibility that he was not unconscious?
Loubser	No.

Witness: Prof. Simpson

He believed that after a head injury of the type sustained by Biko there would have been a significant change in the level of consciousness. He would be very surprised if, according to evidence led, the injury to Biko's left forehead occurred with no loss of consciousness. It was impossible to be dogmatic, but he would find it surprising if Biko sustained his brain lesions without loss of consciousness.

| Prins | At what stage would Biko have passed the point of no return? |

Prof. Simpson thought this was very shortly after sustaining his head injury. He believed it was probably within six to eight hours after this had occurred.

| Prof. Oliver (Assessor) | Was it possible to give an indication of the amount of force necessary to cause the head injury? |

Prof. Simpson thought it would have needed a fair amount of localised force.

Witness: Prof. Proctor

There was considerable evidence to indicate that brain injury would result in unconsciousness.

| Kentridge | On the morning of 7 September Mr. Biko had been difficult to make contact with, did not answer questions, was incoherent, displayed indications of ataxia (staggering gait); the following day he had a weakness of his left side, showed the extensor plantar reflex and the morning after that red cells were found in his cerebral spinal fluid. Given this picture, would the injuries suffered have resulted in immediate unconsciousness? |
| Proctor | From this picture with the nature and extent of Biko's injuries, he must have been unconscious. Biko had suffered moderate to severe brain damage. In the case of moderate injury I estimate that 10 to 20 minutes unconsciousness was reasonable. |

70

He had grave doubts, considering the extent of injuries, that Biko could have been only momentarily unconscious.

*   *   *

The next point to determine was the time and date of the injury.

Witness: Prof. Loubser

Kentridge   The visible injury on Mr. Biko's forehead consisted of a bruise, swelling and scab shown on a photograph before the court.

Professor Loubser said he had conducted an ageing test on this wound and estimated it was between four and eight days old.

Kentridge   This wound must then have been suffered before the night of 8 September?

Loubser   If my maths serves me well, yes.

Kentridge   The date of his death was 12 September; taking five days back would be 7 September and six days back would take us to 6 September?

Loubser   Such a period of time lapse would be applicable.

On examining the body, Loubser added, he immediately observed the injury on Biko's forehead. He had no difficulty in seeing the wound.

Van Rooyen   My advisers say that the age of this injury could make a difference to the visibility?

Loubser   This kind of injury takes on a brown colour and becomes visible when it is dried by the atmosphere. My view is that it should have been visible within the first few hours.

Van Rooyen   You looked at it post-mortem. It is possible that more visibility developed after death?

Loubser   Yes.

Van Rooyen   In the photographic process the reflection can also accent the contrast?

Loubser   I saw the wound itself, not the photograph, and for me it was an extremely visible lesion. I saw and described the wound before it was photographed.

Van Rooyen   My problem is that a large number of people saw Mr. Biko in life but with the exception of one, none of them admitted under oath to having seen the wound. It is possible that in life the wound was not obvious?

Loubser   I have found that I, too, in doing post-mortems have missed lesions because of the subjective factor.

Witness: Prof. Proctor

He had estimated contusions in the brain to be at least three to five days old at the date of the post-mortem, 13 September.

12 days was much more likely than 15 as the outside limit of the age of the lesion, but he would agree with Prof. Loubser that a period of five to eight days was the closest one could get to a reasonable analysis of the age of the lesion.

He believed that the lesions were of the same age, but could not say they were inflicted simultaneously.

Van Rooyen   Unconsciousness can happen in a wide variety of degrees?

Proctor   Yes. Even with severe brain damage, the degree of unconsciousness could be slight.

Van Rooyen   You were in the field of sheer speculation when you mentioned that Biko should have been unconscious for up to 15 minutes?

Proctor   I have come to appreciate that unconsciousness is an essential factor in brain damage. Here is a case of brain damage. This patient would have been unconscious in the medical sense.

Kentridge   What was the likelihood of unconsciousness in Biko's case?

Proctor   After considering the number, extent, and nature of the lesions in the brain, and the physical history, I believe Biko was unconscious.

❖   ❖   ❖

The other injuries to Biko's body were also considered, although it was clear that these had not been the cause of death.

Witness: Prof. Loubser

He could not tie the two lip injuries with the other head injuries. It seemed to him the lip injuries were quite separate. He agreed with Mr. Kentridge that the cuts on the lip were more likely to have been caused by two blows than a fall.

Kentridge   Turning to the bruising of the rib area. These injuries showed they were probably caused by a jab with a sharp object for example a finger or a stick?

Loubser   Agreed. It wasn't a vicious jab it was just a jab.

Kentridge   And the abrasions found on Mr. Biko's wrists and feet?

Loubser believed they were caused by handcuffs and manacles. He had found a wound on Mr. Biko's left big toe, what appeared to have been a blister with a small hole in it caused by something like a 'pin or needle'.

Kentridge   What could have caused it?

Loubser believed it was a mechanical cause . . . a bump or pressure at that point.

❖   ❖   ❖

Besides dealing with the head injury, the pathologists present at the post-mortem were also questioned on other matters. The following evidence is taken from the testimony of the doctor who attended the post-mortem on behalf of the Biko family. His presence had been agreed by the Chief State Pathologist, Professor Loubser.

72

Witness: Dr. Jonathan Gluckman, Pathologist, for the Biko Family.

Although not regarding himself as a specialist neuropathologist, Gluckman had studied the conclusions reached by Prof. Proctor and was completely satisfied with them.

Kentridge   Referring to injuries found on Biko's left big toe which had the appearance of a blister which had been pierced; could you throw light on them?

Gluckman   None whatsoever. It was a source of considerable speculation. I don't think any of us was able to give a reasonable background to the injuries. It was most peculiar.

When he arrived at the post-mortem, Biko's scalp had been opened up. He observed the bruising within the scalp. It was very striking indeed. Biko's skin colouring was darker than that on the photograph handed in to the Court.

Kentridge   Allowing for that, can you explain why in the days before his death it wasn't seen by the doctors and others who saw him?

Gluckman   It is beyond my comprehension.

On the question of dating the head injuries, Gluckman agreed with Prof. Loubser that it fell between four and eight days before Mr. Biko's death. He believed it was nearer five or six days than four or eight days.

Kentridge   Will you, as a pathologist, comment on the report of the lumbar puncture?

Gluckman   This report has contradictions. The analysis reports show the spinal fluid to be colourless, and at the same time containing 1655 red cells. Spinal fluid containing this count could not possibly have been clear. Anything from 200 to 300 red cells is slightly turbid, and this increases as the number of red cells increases. It is not possible to have fluid containing over 1600 red cells, and for that fluid to be clear. One or other is incorrect.

Gluckman added that the tests for xanthrochromia, which would indicate brain damage, had proved negative.

Gluckman   As I reject absolutely the statement that the fluid was clear, so must I reject that there was no xanthochromia. Clearly the observation was faulty.

Kentridge   Who signed the report?

Gluckman   The signature was illegible, but a rubber stamp bore the name 'Nelis'.

Kentridge   What should be the reaction of a physician receiving such a report?

Gluckman   I wouldn't accept it. Alternatively, the lumbar puncture should be repeated because of the paradoxical result.

Kentridge   A false name, Stephen Njelo, appeared on Mr. Biko's lumbar puncture analysis form. According to accepted medical practice,

	where does the responsibility lie for putting the name of the patient on the sample that is sent?
Gluckman	There can be no equivocation. It lies solely in the hands of the doctor in charge of the case. It cannot be delegated.
Kentridge	Dr. Tucker told the court that the Hippocratic Oath had a bearing on his ethical conduct, but that his conduct was actually governed by the rules of the SA Medical and Dental Council.
Gluckman	I was somewhat surprised at this. There is nothing in the Hippocratic Oath that conflicts with the rules of the Medical and Dental Council. The ethical component of the rule is a legal codification of the principles fundamental to Hippocratic Oath. In terms of accepted medical ethics, the interest of the patient—and nothing else—is paramount to the doctor.

Mr. Van Rooyen then questioned Dr. Gluckman about the lumbar puncture performed on Biko before his death.

Van Rooyen	Dr. Colin Hersch, a Port Elizabeth specialist, has told the court that macroscopically (to the naked eye) the fluid had appeared clear.
Gluckman	It could not have been so. The reports were patently contradictory.
Van Rooyen	You don't know which of the two reports, that the fluid was clear or that it had a count of 1655 red blood cells, was correct?
Gluckman	Agreed.
Prof. Gordon	The point is that the fluid went to the institute under the name of Njelo. I don't even know if the fluid was the correct fluid. For me that wipes out the whole thing.
Gluckman	As far as I'm concerned the report from the institute is only for the wastepaper basket. It contradicts itself. If it is not faulty in one respect it is faulty in another respect. We pathologists are critical of laboratory tests because such a lot depends on observation. At a glance I would say the report is nonsense.
Van Rooyen	Let us put ourselves in the Port Elizabeth context. The doctor who made the lumbar puncture said the fluid was clear and the report stated that the fluid was clear. Would that doctor not be entitled to accept the report?
Gluckman	It cannot be clear if there are 1655 red blood cells in it.

Questioned by Mr. Pickard (for the doctors), Dr. Gluckman said that if the report had stated that the fluid was turbid he would have accepted it.

Pickard	You have told the Court that you were concerned about the fact that the report from the medical institute had not been signed by a pathologist?
Gluckman	I am concerned.

Dr. Gluckman said that the test had probably been done by a technologist but that such a test was always signed by a pathologist in clinical laboratories, showing that a pathologist had scrutinised the report.

Pickard   Do you suggest that Dr. Hersch should have known that the report was not signed by a pathologist?

Gluckman   I presume it is normal procedure in Port Elizabeth for a pathologist not to sign the report. Otherwise Dr. Hersch would have questioned it.

Prins   I can see your point that the report should be signed by a qualified practitioner. But can you say that any general practitioner would check the signature?

Gluckman   That is a very difficult question but a general practitioner must be in a position to phone the pathologists to discuss the tests. Even an indecipherable squiggle is often recognisable.

Pickard   We are now trying to determine if anybody was responsible for the death of Steve Biko. I assume that you came to court with the object of assisting it in that respect. Was the suggestion about the signature raised merely to build a case against Dr. Hersch?

Gluckman   I must protest in the strongest terms. I cannot blame Dr. Hersch for not being hypercritical of reports issued by the medical institute. I merely say that I am very critical.

Pickard   Are you criticising the South African Institute for Medical Research?

Gluckman   The high-sounding name means nothing. A report is only as good as the man who signs it.

Pickard   Surely it is as good as the technician who did it?

Gluckman   The pathologist has to supervise his staff closely. I would not be prepared to have my head opened on a technologist's report in the absence of a pathologist's confirmation.

Pickard   What is your opinion of the South African Institute for Medical Research?

Gluckman   I am of the opinion that the Institute employs some very competent individuals, some of medium competence and some who are not so competent.

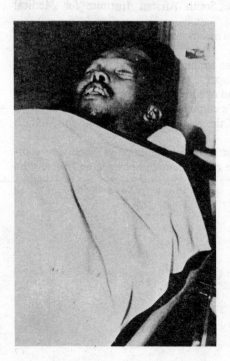
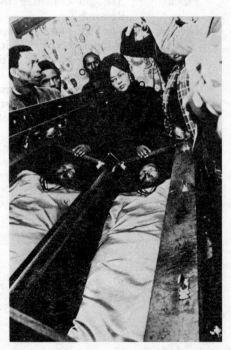

Magistrate M. J. Prins

Major H. Snyman

Minister of Police J. Kruger

Colonel P. Goosen

Lieut. W. Wilken

Crowds at the funeral

Ntsiki Biko, Steve Biko's widow

Biko's young son Samora among mourners

IX

The Doctors

After receiving his head injury, Biko began to die. According to Professor Proctor, 'treatment might have prevented his death from oedema'. According to Professor Ian Simpson, Biko passed the point of no return within six to eight hours after sustaining his head injury.

It was thus important to establish from the doctors who saw Biko between 7 September and his death on 12 September why no effective medical treatment was given. But, like the police, the doctors giving evidence presented testimony that was neither disinterested nor frank.

Witness: Dr. Ivor Lang, District Surgeon, Port Elizabeth.

Since the death of Biko he had made a number of statements. At first he said simply that at the request of Col. Goosen he had examined Biko on 7 September in the offices of the Security Police about 12 noon.

He had signed the following statement:

This is to certify that I have examined Steve Biko as a result of a request from Col. Goosen of the Security Police who complained that the above-mentioned would not speak.

I have found no evidence of any abnormality or pathology on detainee.

In a later affidavit, signed on 1 October, he said that the time 12 noon was incorrect and that he had in fact examined Mr. Biko at 9.20 a.m. In court Lang continued: Later that day, 7 September, Col. Goosen had expressed concern that Biko might have suffered a stroke since he was not eating 'nor was he able to speak and was not using his limbs'.

Lang had agreed to re-examine Biko later in the morning and had requested the Chief District Surgeon, Dr. B. J. Tucker, to examine with him.

This examination started at 12.45 p.m. in the Security Police offices.

Lang   I carried out a lengthy and complete examination of Biko who was lying in an office on a number of blankets. He was able to give me a good account of himself and did not complain of any symptoms other than weakness of his limbs and lacked the desire to eat.

I informed Col. Goosen I could find no organic cause for Mr. Biko's apparent weakness and I was satisfied that he had not suffered a stroke.

The next morning, 8 September, Col. Goosen expressed concern over Biko's condition since he had not passed urine during the previous 24 hours and he had refused all offers of food.

He had re-examined Biko, and noted no material changes in his physical condition save for the facts set out in his medical report.

Lang   There was certainly no distension of his bladder and no indication that he was suffering from retention of urine. At the conclusion of this examination Biko complained of thirst whereupon Warrant Officer Coetzee was asked to give him water.

In view of our observations it was decided that he be transferred to the Sydenham Prison Hospital where a further examination could be carried out by a specialist physician and this was immediately agreed to by Col. Goosen.

Kentridge   The certificate written after your examination on 7 September said you found no evidence of any abnormality or pathology on Biko.

Lang said he had been asked to make out a certificate at Col. Goosen's request. He presumed it was 'merely for record purposes'.

Kentridge   Didn't it occur to you that if, at some later stage, Biko might appear in court and complain about the way he was treated while in Security Police custody, your medical certificate would be a most important piece of evidence?

Lang   Correct.

Lang added that the thought did not occur to him on 7 September.

Kentridge   In your original certificate for Col. Goosen you only mentioned the fact that Biko 'would not speak' as the reason why a medical examination was ordered. In the report to the pathologist conducting the post mortem, you gave the reason as follows: 'The detainee had refused water and food and displayed a weakness of all four limbs and it was feared that he had suffered a stroke'. In your certificate you only said he would not speak. Why were the other matters not in your certificate?

Lang   I cannot explain it. It is inexplicable.

Kentridge   Being wanted for record purposes wasn't it important to have a complete and correct record?

Lang   In retrospect, yes.

Kentridge   You wrote: 'I have found no evidence of any abnormality or pathology on the detainee'.

Lang replied that in fact he had found a small laceration on Biko's lip, a bruise near his second rib, two swollen hands, swollen feet and ankles.

Kentridge   None of this is mentioned in your certificate. Wouldn't a person who later read your certificate have taken it to mean there was no sign of injury on Biko—so that part was also highly incorrect?

Lang   Yes, it was.

Kentridge	It may have been that Biko would one day have said he had a cut, bruised, swollen lip and he would have been called a liar?
Lang	I see that now.
Kentridge	Isn't that why Col. Goosen wanted the certificate?
Lang	I don't think so.

In his examination of 7 September, Lang noticed Biko's speech was slurred, which he attributed to the lip injury, and that he had a staggering gait which he attributed to lack of co-operation.

Kentridge	You were aware of Biko's history—that he had studied medicine for four years, and later studied commerce and law?
Lang	I was initially informed of these facts by Col. Goosen, which were later confirmed by Biko himself.
Kentridge	Isn't it fairly clear that Col. Goosen stressed the fact that Biko had been a medical student as a hint to you he might be shamming?
Lang	It is a probability.
Kentridge	Did you question Biko?
Lang	Yes.
Kentridge	Did you ask how he got the cut on his lip and the bruises on his chest?
Lang	No.
Kentridge	Why not?
Lang	Because I was told by Col. Goosen that Biko had gone into a rage and had attempted to assault an officer with a chair and had to be restrained.

He had assumed that the lip injury and the bruises had been sustained while the police were trying to control Biko. Biko had not complained of being injured or assaulted.

Kentridge	Why did you make an assumption?
Lang	I think if Biko had not been injured as a result of restraint, Col. Goosen would have told me.
Kentridge	Would he? Had Goosen been present?
Lang	Col. Goosen was present for about half the examination.
Kentridge	Why did you not ask Biko for his version of the event while Col. Goosen was out of the room?
Lang	I assumed Biko would have told me himself.
Kentridge	Were you not reluctant to embarrass Col. Goosen?
Lang	No.
Kentridge	Didn't the possibility of a head injury occur to you?
Lang	Yes, immediately. The moment I saw the lip injury this was uppermost in my mind.
Kentridge	Why didn't you ask any question about it?
Lang	I can't answer that.

78

Kentridge	Col. Goosen never said anything to you to suggest that Biko had a bump on his head?
Lang	No. No Security Police officer ever mentioned the possibility. My examination was to a certain extent dependent on the history of the patient given to me. If I had not been told a full and correct history I could well have been put off the track.
Kentridge	Did you order the leg irons not to be replaced due to the swelling on Biko's ankle?

Lang said he had not thought of it at the time but in retrospect would have recommended it.

Kentridge	On 7 September did you think Mr. Biko was malingering?

Lang said his findings as well as the history he had been given on Biko led to that conclusion. He had been told Biko could not speak and yet he had held a conversation with him.

Kentridge	What sort of feigning is it that stops the moment a doctor comes in and in the presence of a colonel? Isn't it odd?
Lang	It is odd.
Kentridge	May I suggest that the suggestion of feigning was very largely derived from Col. Goosen?
Lang	It contributed to it.

Lang believed Biko's slurred speech could definitely be attributed to the lip injury. He had not prescribed any treatment for it because the cut was 'extremely superficial'.

He attributed Biko's staggering (ataxic) gait to the fact that he had been manacled and his ankles were swollen.

Kentridge	Why in your report to the pathologist did you attribute Biko's staggering to 'a lack of co-operation'. A person reading this would understand it as a deliberate failure to co-operate. You agree that this is misleading?
Lang	Yes, I agree.
Kentridge	A report made by Col. Goosen and Maj. Snyman said that Biko's speech was not merely slurred but incoherent?
Lang	'Thick speech' was a more adequate description than the phrase 'slurred speech'.
Kentridge	And after the medical examination Mr. Biko was left lying on his mat in the office in chains?
Lang	I had examined Biko very carefully and found nothing 'emphatically' wrong with him.
Kentridge	Why did you not order Biko to be kept in bed, in view of the symptoms you had noticed?

Dr. Lang replied that he had told Col. Goosen that if Mr. Biko's condition persisted he should be called again.

8 September

On the following day, 8 September, Lang was again called by Col. Goosen to examine Biko with the Chief District Surgeon, Dr. Tucker. Biko was coherent.

Kentridge   There are many witnesses who have said that after a certain period Biko was incoherent and that they could not make contact with him.

Lang   Biko replied clearly when asked his name.

Kentridge said he had been instructed that questioning on that level was not an adequate test of the degree of consciousness or mental ability.

Kentridge   The fact that Mr. Biko was in chains was not mentioned until your fourth affidavit. Didn't you think it necessary to mention that in your original report?

Lang   No. I didn't mention it. Biko was still lying on the mat chained by his one foot. I cannot remember whether Biko was handcuffed. I was not told that Biko had been violent again.

Before commencing the examination the doctors were told by Col. Goosen that Biko had not passed urine for 24 hours. They found on examination that his blankets were wet with urine and that they were smelling.

Kentridge   Was nothing done about that?

Lang   Not while we were there.

Kentridge   Biko might have spent some time under the wet blanket?

Lang   He might have.

At the end of that examination Biko had asked for water because he was thirsty and had been given it by a member of the security staff.

He did not accept Col. Goosen's story that Biko had not passed urine, because he had wet his bed. There was no sign of dehydration about Biko.

Dr. Lang went on to speak of a second examination of Biko on 8 September when Biko had complained of vague pains in his head and back.

Dr. Tucker said he had found a doubtful 'possible extensor plantar reflex'. This meant that when stroked on the sole of his foot, instead of his toes curling inwards, there was a sign that his big toe might be turning upwards. Dr. Tucker then said they wanted to take Biko to hospital in order that a specialist could examine him.

Kentridge   At this stage did you think he was shamming?

Lang   I couldn't understand why he had passed urine in the bed. My only conclusion was that he couldn't get up. I asked him and he couldn't give me a satisfactory answer.

Kentridge   What was done when Biko complained of a pain in his head?

Lang   Biko was very vague about this.

Kentridge   Did you still think of the possibility of his having a head injury?

Lang   It was in the back of my mind.

Kentridge   It might have been at the back of your mind but it was not in the forefront of your affidavit.

Kentridge returned to Goosen's suggestion that Biko was feigning.

Kentridge   Had Col. Goosen put you under the impression that during Biko's last period of detention he had manifested the same symptoms? If this were false, would he not have been seriously misleading the medical practitioners?

Lang agreed. Had he not been given the information about Biko's previous behaviour in detention his approach to his diagnosis might have been different: it might not have led to the conclusion that Biko was shamming. On 7 September he examined Mr. Biko's head very carefully.

Kentridge   It seems inconceivable that you didn't see the injury.

Lang   I did not see it. I have no cause to hide the fact. I can offer no explanation. I examined his pupils and noticed a swelling on his upper lip but I saw no injury.

Had Biko looked the way he had looked in the photograph with the scab he would have seen it.

Kentridge   Isn't it perhaps the case that just as you omitted to mention in your report the chest injury and the lip injury you omitted the head injury?

Lang   I saw the lip injury and the chest injury. I can assure you that the chest injury was not that obvious.

Here even Mr. van Rooyen appeared to feel that Lang's evidence was verging on the incredible, and intervened in his support:

Van Rooyen   I suppose you have been lying awake at nights, worrying since Biko's death?

Lang   Very many nights.

Van Rooyen   On the morning of the 7th when you were called in did Col. Goosen make it clear that he had been concerned about Biko's health?

Lang   This is correct. Col. Goosen had stressed his concern.

Van Rooyen   Did he say he would give his right arm for the life of this detainee?

Lang   I heard this at the time. It was quite clear that Col. Goosen was concerned about Biko's good health.

The second doctor to give evidence was Dr. Lang's senior colleague.

Witness: Dr. Benjamin Tucker, Chief District Surgeon, Port Elizabeth.

At his examination on 8 September, Tucker said he did not think Biko was incontinent but that because of his position he had been unable to move.

Kentridge   Because he was chained up? Did you call Col. Goosen's attention to this?

Tucker   No. Col. Goosen had said Biko hadn't asked to go to the toilet.

Kentridge   Wasn't he your patient at this stage?

Tucker   Yes.

Kentridge	Were you not interested why your patient, a grown man, should have wet his bed?
Tucker	I was.
Kentridge	Why didn't you ask him?
Tucker	I cannot answer.
Kentridge	There is only one answer, you knew he couldn't answer you.
Tucker	I'm afraid that is incorrect.
Kentridge	Did you ask Biko how he cut his lip?
Tucker	I did not.
Kentridge	What sort of doctor is it who doesn't ask a patient how he got his injury?
Tucker	Col. Goosen told me that Biko became aggressive, had to be restrained and I assumed that the lip injury was the result of this restraint.
Kentridge	You assumed it?
Tucker	I accepted that in the restraint there must have been a struggle and that Biko by some means could have injured his lip.
Kentridge	By what means?
Tucker	I don't know what means were used.
Kentridge	Why didn't you ask?
Tucker	Because this was an assumption I thought I was entitled to make.
Kentridge	What right have you got to make any assumption? Why didn't you ask him?
	Reply inaudible.
Kentridge	In your affidavit there is a statement that there were abrasions around both wrists. The affidavit was a copy of a medical report and I would have thought you had a duty in the medical report to note any possible reason for the abrasions. Why was there no explanation for the abrasions?
Tucker	I did not think it was necessary.
Kentridge	Why didn't you say he was handcuffed and his leg shackled to a grille?

Tucker replied that he had done this in his second affidavit. Biko's hands were free and he was only shackled around his right ankle. He accepted that the abrasions on the wrists were due to previous handcuffs.

Kentridge	You didn't mention it in your medical report for fear of embarrassing the Security Branch?
Tucker	This is an assumption I just cannot accept.

He agreed that he had not made mention in the medical report of abrasions on Biko's feet and ankle.

Had he left them out because any mention of these abrasions would have pointed to the fact that Mr. Biko had been manacled?

Tucker	It was an error.

Kentridge	Supposing Biko had lived and had come to court and complained he had been chained by his ankle, your report would have been produced and it would have been put to him that he could not have been because otherwise you would have noticed it?
Tucker	If the question had been asked.
Kentridge	Your statement says that at no time did Biko mention that he had been assaulted or injured. You were aware that Biko had a lip injury. Did you not know about the chest injury as well?

Tucker said he did not but that Dr. Lang had mentioned the bruise on the chest. He could not find it.

Kentridge	What is the value of saying Biko had not been injured in any way when you can see an injury on him?
Tucker	He had not volunteered this information to me.
Kentridge	You didn't see fit to ask him? You just made an assumption?
Tucker	Yes.

Tucker added that he had asked him whether he had any complaints and Biko said he had a headache and a pain in the back. He had asked no other questions.

Kentridge	You asked him one question and you got one answer. Was that the sum total of the questions?
Tucker	Yes.

He added that he could not recall Dr. Lang asking any more questions.

Kentridge	On that basis you say in your affidavit: 'He was alert but answered questions in an indistinct manner'. This is a misleading statement.
Tucker	I am sorry.
Kentridge	It is not merely misleading, it is a plainly false statement.
Tucker	I cannot say that.
Kentridge	Well, I can. I will tell you why. He didn't answer questions. At most he answered one question. And secondly, on the basis of that single question and answer you had no right to say that mentally he was alert.

The questioning moved on to the subject of brain damage.

Tucker stated that the upgoing big toe on the right side was not clear but might have indicated a neurological problem.

Kentridge	You say you had in mind the possibility of a head injury?
Tucker	Yes.
Kentridge	If someone said this man had bumped his head against the wall, would you have taken a different view?
Tucker	No.
Kentridge	If you had the suspicion that he had some neurological damage and you knew he was in some sort of violent incident, would you not have asked whether he had received a blow on the head? *Reply inaudible.*

Kentridge	I am suggesting to you that the reason you did not ask was because you were dealing with the Security Police.
Tucker	No.

Mr. van Rooyen at this stage objected strongly to Kentridge's statement.

Kentridge	It is a question, not a statement. Why don't you ask a question in that situation?
Tucker	I would say no you don't.

Tucker's admission caused noisy murmuring in the packed court room. The Magistrate, Mr. Prins, called an adjournment for five minutes. When the Court re-assembled, Tucker attempted to retract his statement.

Tucker	I would like to rephrase my reply.
Kentridge	I thought you were agreeing with me.
Tucker	My answer to the question is: No, it is not so. Questions asked by the district surgeon are not banned in the security offices.
Kentridge	I don't suggest they are banned. I suggest that you personally did not ask the question.
Tucker	I can only object strongly. At all times I have always had all the co-operation necessary from the Security Police.
Kentridge	You used the word 'co-operation'. What co-operation? What does co-operation mean?
Tucker	You used it. My meaning of the word is that when we require information and when we require things to be done, then they are done.
Kentridge	You deny you have any inhibitions asking them questions even if they embarrass them?
Tucker	Yes.
Kentridge	Why did you not ask whether Biko got a bump on the head? Did Goosen at no stage say to you that this man had received a bump on his head?
Tucker	No.
Kentridge	Nor did any other officer say that to you?
Tucker	No.
Kentridge	Did anyone suggest to you that Biko had received a bump on the head?
Tucker	Gen. Kleinhaus.
Kentridge	When?
Tucker	At the time of the interview [on 19 October].
Kentridge	That was the first time it was suggested to you?
Tucker	Also when I spoke to Prof. Loubser the Chief State Pathologist in Pretoria, on the following morning, probably the 13 September.
Kentridge	When you last saw Biko was he still on the same mat under a wet blanket with the same trousers on?
Tucker	Yes. I gave no orders in that regard.

think of the possibility that the man had suffered a
?
ly mind.
ask Biko any questions about it?

No.

Kentridge   Didn't you ask Col. Goosen any questions about it?

Tucker   No. I thought the injury to his lip might have caused a brain injury.

Kentridge   Dr. Tucker, if you thought the lip injury was evidence of a head injury, oughtn't you to have gone into it further?

Tucker   From whom? From Col. Goosen? I don't think I can reply. There was this history of restraint and the injury could have come from that period.

Kentridge   Why did you not ask the obvious question, whether the man received a bump on the head?

Tucker   I did not ask it and that is all I can say.

Prins   Did you ask Biko?

Tucker   No.

Kentridge   Was it not possible you were reluctant to embarrass Goosen?

Tucker   No.

Kentridge   Either from reading about it or from your own experience have you no knowledge that the police assault people in custody?

Tucker   I have. (*Further answer inaudible*).

Kentridge   But on that occasion you did not ask?

Tucker   No, I did not. Where persons are brought to me for examination my report is completed on a special form. This is all I am required to do. The history was given to Dr. Lang . . . the restraint could have resulted in the damage.

Kentridge   You accept it as a fact, what Goosen told you?

Tucker   May I put it this way? If I am called to see a patient and he has a cut on his head, then I am interested in treating him and not in how he got the cut.

Kentridge   In the interest in treating the patient, is it not also essential and wise to know what caused it?

Tucker   There was the history that Biko had become hysterical and that he had to be restrained . . .

Kentridge   Why should it not have been caused by the brain injury?

Tucker   Dr. Lang said there were no signs of bruises around the head.

Kentridge   Let me start again. You are a professional man and you are not doing yourself justice. Are you not aware that sometimes there are cases of people assaulted in custody? Did you not think about it?

Tucker   No.

Dr. Tucker was then cross-examined by Van Rooyen.

85

Van Rooyen	The man was complaining of various things, there was also Goosen's worry about the man and his condition of health, and you felt it would be best to have him examined by a specialist?
Tucker	That is correct.
Van Rooyen	In case you were missing something, let's have a specialist look at it?
Tucker	Well, Your Worship, the two of us had found different signs and we wanted another opinion.
Van Rooyen	Yes, and therefore you suggested that in order to get a specialist's opinion it would be advisable to have him taken to a hospital where he could be observed and be examined?
Tucker	That is correct.
Van Rooyen	It wasn't as if you had an ill man on your hands, doctor? Obviously ill?
Tucker	Not at that particular stage.
Van Rooyen	In your mind you at no time even thought that you had here on your hands a sick man?
Tucker	Not in the slightest.

At this stage, Prof. Gordon, one of the assessors, intervened.

Gordon	You know, this is surprising. I am sorry to interrupt you, but how can you say that you did not have on your hands a sick man, and yet you say that it is necessary to have a consultant to see him at a hospital? It just does not make sense to me. If your man is not sick, then you don't need a hospital, and you don't need a specialist.

I am trying to work out what your reasoning process was. If your reasoning process was, we don't even have a sick man on our hands Col. Goosen, don't worry about it. But you don't do that. You say, we don't even have a sick man on our hands, but nonetheless we will have a consultant's opinion and we will try and get that in a hospital. |
| *Tucker* | Yes, and we would feel far happier. |
| *Gordon* | You see, because it is nonsense to talk this way. I am sorry to put it to you like that . . . you are a doctor . . . It is just that it is unimpressive to me. |

*   *   *

Like Lang, Tucker virtually admitted that he had simply followed security police instructions when examining Biko and had ordered no treatment; although it was agreed that Biko be transferred to Sydenham Prison for further investigation.

This took place on 8 September.

86

Witness: Dr. Lang

During the afternoon of 8 September, Dr. Hersch, consultant physician, was contacted and agreed to examine Biko in consultation with Lang during the evening.

Biko was moved to Sydenham Prison for the examination.

About 9.45 p.m. Dr. Hersch examined Biko in Lang's presence at the Sydenham Prison and it was agreed that a lumbar puncture be performed the next morning to exclude the possibility of cerebral haemorrhage or other cerebral disease.

von Lieres   You were unable to make a diagnosis and therefore you couldn't have told Col. Goosen Mr. Biko was a sick man?

Lang   No I didn't.

von Lieres   Would Col. Goosen have allowed Biko to be hospitalised if you had reported Biko to be very ill?

Dr. Lang replied that this was a difficult question to answer. He got the impression that under no circumstances would Biko be allowed to go into hospital.

von Lieres   What would the situation have been if a definite diagnosis had been made?

Lang believed that if he had told Col. Goosen there was positive information that Biko was definitely ill, he would have been sent to hospital.

9 September

A lumbar puncture was performed by Dr. Hersch on the morning of 9 September. About 9.45 a.m. Lang visited Biko.

Lang   He was comfortable and did not complain of any pain and was in possession of all his faculties. I received a report from Warder Shehab to the effect that Biko had eaten half a plate of food and that he was found in a bath of water during the early hours of the morning and that all his clothing was soaking wet.

    Shortly after this I telephoned Dr. Hersch who informed me that the lumbar puncture was performed with little difficulty but that the cerebro-spinal fluid, although not under pressure, was bloodstained. Furthermore, there was no change in Biko's physical condition.

10 September

On the morning of 10 September, Dr. Lang again consulted Dr. Hersch on the phone and the report of the analysis of cerebral haemorrhage was discussed.

Because of the presence of blood Dr. Hersch was of the opinion that a neurosurgeon be consulted and if necessary an X-ray of the skull be obtained. Lang gave his consent.

Shortly after this Mr. R. Keeley, a neuro-surgeon, telephoned him and Biko's clinical state was discussed at length. Keeley was of the opinion that the findings to date were not evidence of cerebral haemorrhage or for that matter any other brain damage, that an X-ray would not be of much value, and that it was his opinion that all that was necessary at this stage would be observation. 'Keeley agreed that we could transfer him to the custody of the Security Police provided that he was examined daily by a doctor'.

Lang advised Col. Goosen of this. It was agreed that Biko would be moved from Sydenham Prison the next morning.

At 3.30 p.m. he again visited Biko and found him comfortable with no complaints and no change in his physical condition. 'I received a report that he had flung the plate of food off the bed on to the floor with his hands at midday. I informed Biko of the findings of the various medical practitioners and that he was to be moved from Sydenham Prison the following morning'.

In cross-examination Kentridge inquired about the medical examination:

Kentridge	You were present when the plantar reflex was tested. You reported wrongly that it was tested on the right. It should have been on the left?
Lang	Yes.
Kentridge	Yet you say in your bed letter that both Dr. Hersch and you could find no pathology. That was false?
Lang	Yes.
Kentridge	And that the lumbar puncture was normal. That was false?
Lang	No, it was incorrect.
Kentridge	It was false to say that no pathology could be found?
Lang	I gave an incorrect statement in the bed letter. There was an omission of one word. It should have read gross pathology. This was the essence of what I told Biko. That there was no indication of gross pathology.
Kentridge	This was also false. A most significant sign of brain injury had been found.
Lang	To my mind the upgoing toe was only one of a few.
Kentridge	I am going to suggest that it is perfectly clear that you made a false statement to Biko and in your bed letter to get Biko back to the hands of the police as soon as possible.
Lang	I deny that. It was an error on my part.

The same events were also recounted by Dr. Hersch.

Witness: Dr. Colin Hersch, Consultant Physician, Port Elizabeth

On 8 September, Hersch was phoned by Dr. Lang and given the history of Biko. Biko had shown difficulty in talking and had dragged his left leg. Dr. Lang also mentioned the possibility of an upgoing toe on the right foot.

Hersch suspected Biko was shamming. He later also gained the impression from Col. Goosen that Biko might be shamming, although Col. Goosen was keen for him to rule out the possibility of a stroke. At no stage did Col. Goosen mention the possibility that Biko might have had a bump on his head, although he did mention the episode where Biko allegedly threw a chair at an officer and had to be restrained.

Hersch said he got the message that he was dealing with a man who might be feigning and that he was a dangerous man.

Kentridge   They didn't leave it to your skill and judgement to report?

Hersch   I got that history quite clear. Particularly in neurological cases a wrong history could prejudice the examination.

Hersch claimed that he never noticed the bruise on Biko's head or the scab that was apparent in the post-mortem photograph. 'But in retrospect I have quite a clear picture of him standing with a whitish area over his left eye that I thought was dry saliva or sputum'. He did not think he could have missed an abrasion had there been one.

Kentridge   How do you account for the fact that it wasn't seen?

Hersch   I really don't know. By the rest of the examination one could almost have expected it to be there. It fitted in with indications of brain injury that there should have been a lesion there.

Dealing with the plantar reflex, Hersch admitted that the upgoing toe on the left side was a significant sign. It showed a great likelihood of organic brain damage. Dr. Lang had observed the upgoing toe as well. The upgoing toe changed the whole picture of Biko's condition.

Afterwards he had explained to Col. Goosen that there were positive findings of something wrong with the nervous system. 'I don't remember the actual words. I made it clear there were positive findings'.

Hersch agreed that Biko's poor co-operation would have been due to brain damage, and denied that he had ever expressed the opinion to Col. Goosen that Biko might be shamming or that he had given Dr. Lang the all clear after the investigation.

The result of the lumbar puncture left any conclusion on Biko's condition 'wide open', according to Hersch. The blood cells could have been due to a brain injury or a bloody tap—blood drawn from blood vessels, not the spinal fluid. But the ease with which a lumbar puncture was performed was a point against the possibility of a bloody tap.

Notwithstanding the fact that he suspected damage on the brain, he did not mention this specifically in his medical report.

Kentridge   On the form sent with Biko's spinal fluid to the Institute for Medical Research for testing the name of the patient was made out as Stephen Njelo. Was a false name filled in so the staff at the Institute would not know the patient's real name?

Hersch replied that he did not know who filled in the name on the form. It might have been an orderly at the Sydenham Prison Hospital. 'I don't know who it was', he said.

Kentridge	Isn't it the doctor's responsibility to label the specimen bottle?
Hersch	I do not know who did it. A male nurse helped with the lumbar puncture.

Kentridge said he tried to find out from the Institute whether they had done tests on Biko's spinal fluid and at first got a negative reply. He then returned to Hersch's own report.

Kentridge	A bed letter written by Dr. Lang on 10 September said that he and Dr. Hersch could find no pathology on Biko and that the lumbar puncture test was normal. This is absolutely wrong on both counts.

Dr. Hersch agreed they had found signs of pathology in the up-going toe and that there had been blood cells in the spinal fluid which could have pointed to brain injury. 'It was compatible with brain damage as well as compatible with a normal lumbar puncture', he said.

Kentridge	No doctor could say it was normal because of the presence of the red blood cells in the lumbar puncture fluid. When you were examining Biko did you notice a strange wound on his big toe?
Hersch	No.
Kentridge	The post-mortem doctors found a small circular vascular wound 3 mm in diameter as though it had been pricked with an object or a pin?
Hersch	I did not notice it although I have seen the photograph.
Kentridge	Could the wound on the forehead above the left eye have been a substance such as an ointment?
Hersch	I don't think so. I would have seen the mark. I was quite surprised to see the picture.

Despite the medical indications, no treatment was prescribed for Biko at Sydenham Prison, and on 11 September he was taken back into police custody with the doctors' agreement. His condition was clearly deteriorating. He was visited first by Dr. Tucker.

11 September

Witness: Dr. Tucker

Dr. Tucker stated that Col. Goosen had called him in the afternoon of 11 September because he had been on duty and Col. Goosen had been unable to contact Dr. Lang. He was called in because 'evidently something had happened to Biko'. Col. Goosen told him Biko had collapsed and been found by Sergeant Paul Van Vuuren.

Tucker found Biko still lying on the floor in an apathetic condition.

Kentridge	All these people found Biko in a serious enough state to alarm them but you found nothing wrong?
Tucker	I wouldn't say that.

Kentridge	You found froth at the mouth and found that he was hyperventilating. What are the possible causes?
Tucker	Hysteria, renal failure, bleeding of the brain, epileptic seizure, drowning or lung complaints could cause this. I did a rapid new examination.
Kentridge	How rapid?
Tucker	About five minutes.
Kentridge	Did you test for plantar reflex?
Tucker	No.
Kentridge	At the previous examination you found a query. How can you say that the nervous system showed no change?
Tucker	There was essentially no change.

Biko did not stand up during the examination. Tucker tested his legs for spasticity but not for strength or ataxia.

Kentridge	(referring to the photograph taken after Biko's death showing a scab on his forehead). I don't know if you are aware but according to the pathologists the injuries must have been between four and eight days old. It must have been obvious to you as a doctor on Sunday the 11th.
Tucker	It must have been there but it was not visible. I examined both Biko's pupils.
Kentridge	If you examined his left eye with your torch how could you possibly have missed it?
Tucker	The only reason I can give is that it was so insignificant and coloured in the same way as the skin so that I could not distinguish it.
Kentridge	Does it not call into question the thoroughness of your examination?
Tucker	No. Biko was apathetic.
Kentridge	Wasn't it important to establish his level of consciousness?
Tucker	There was a definite uninterestedness.
Kentridge	Why did you do such a cursory examination?
Tucker	I thought I could exclude serious cerebral disease by such an examination. There was no localised sign to indicate to me that any further organic disease was present at the time.
Kentridge	To reach your conclusion you had to ignore the level of consciousness, the plantar reflex and the slight weakness of the left limb? How can you say that there was no sign to indicate organic disease? I put it to you that that was a false statement.
Tucker	An incorrect statement.
Kentridge	Deliberately incorrect?
Tucker	It may have been badly worded.
Kentridge	I say this was a false statement. Won't you concede that?
Tucker	No, I won't.

Kentridge moved on to another area involving Tucker's responsibility as a doctor.

Kentridge You recommended that he should go to a hospital with trained staff and you say Col. Goosen said it was preferable that he should go to a prison hospital. There was no trained staff at the Sydenham Prison Hospital because the only male nurse was on a course and a decision was taken to send Biko to Pretoria. Surely it would have been easier to find a male nurse in Port Elizabeth? Did you argue with Col. Goosen?

Tucker I did not consider Biko's condition to be so serious at that time. I did not insist that he should go into another hospital.

Tucker said he knew that Biko was going to Pretoria in a motor vehicle and had not thought this inadvisable. He did not remonstrate about it. He had not known that Biko was going in a Land Rover but had been told that he was going in a Kombi (Volkswagen mini-bus). He knew that Biko was travelling without any medical attention because there was no male nurse available.

Kentridge In your affidavit you said you did not consider that this journey would have any adverse effect. Did you consider his condition satisfactory?

Tucker I did.

Kentridge You were urgently called in on the Sunday afternoon and told that the man had collapsed. You found him still lying on the floor with froth at his mouth which was unexplained?

Tucker Yes.

Kentridge Similarly, he was hyperventilating but you did not know the cause?

Tucker Yes.

Kentridge You found his left arm somewhat weak?

Tucker Yes.

Kentridge You found him apathetic?

Tucker Yes.

Kentridge You knew that the physician who had examined him had found a plantar reflex?

Tucker Yes.

Kentridge Do you say that a man in that condition could be described as being in a satisfactory condition?

Tucker There was a question in my mind about possible shamming apart from the upgoing toe. There were no other localised features to indicate organic disease.

Kentridge I am going to put it to you that in this situation no honest doctor could have advised that Biko's condition was satisfactory.

Tucker In the circumstances, I thought it was.

Prof. Gordon Why didn't you say that unless Biko goes to hospital you would wipe your hands of the whole affair?

Tucker	I did not think at that stage that Biko's condition would become serious. There was still the question of the possible shamming.
Kentridge	Oh, there was still the possible shamming, was there? Did you think that extensor plantar reflex could be shammed?
Tucker	No.
Kentridge	Did you think that a man could sham red blood cells in the cerebral spinal fluid?
Tucker	No.
Kentridge	In terms of the Hippocratic Oath, to which I take it you subscribe, are not the interests of your patients' paramount?
Tucker	Yes.
Kentridge	But in this instance, they were subordinated to the interests of security? Is that a fair statement?
Tucker	Yes, I didn't know that in this particular situation one could override the decisions made by a responsible police officer.

Dr. Lang corroborated Dr. Tucker's account.

Witness: Dr. Lang

Lang	At 4.45 on 11 September Dr. Tucker telephoned me to report that he had re-examined the detainee. Because Biko was hyperventilating and had not taken any food, I advised that he be transferred to Pretoria Central Prison Hospital either by plane or by road.
	The next morning, on 12 September, about 9.30 a.m. I asked Major Fischer to advise Pretoria that whoever assumed charge of Biko should immediately communicate with Dr. Tucker or myself in order that they be informed of the clinical findings.
Kentridge	At the time when you advised Col. Goosen that a man could go by road to Pretoria you knew that a lumbar puncture had been done but did not know the results?
Lang	Yes.
Kentridge	I am going to submit that in that situation no honest doctor could have advised that Biko's condition was satisfactory.
Lang	In the circumstances I thought it was.
Kentridge	Let us assume a holidaymaker from Pretoria had come to see you in Port Elizabeth about their child who had been acting in a bizarre way. The parents suspected that the child did not want to go back to school, but it showed a plantar reflex, was lying on the floor, had red cells in its spinal fluid, froth at the mouth, was hyperventilating and was weak in the left limbs. Would you have permitted his parents to drive 700 miles to Pretoria?

93

Lang	The circumstances are different. I would have insisted that the child should go into hospital immediately. Here there was an uncertainty.
Kentridge	Shouldn't that have made you more careful rather than less careful? Isn't the only difference that in Biko's case Col. Goosen insisted that he do not go into a hospital?
Lang	I wouldn't say insist. He was averse to the suggestion.
Kentridge	Why didn't you stand up for the interests of your patient?
Lang	I didn't know that in this particular situation one could override the decisions made by a responsible police officer.
Prof. Gordon (Assessor)	Why didn't you say that unless Biko goes to hospital you would wipe your hands of it?
Lang	I did not think at that stage that Biko's condition would become so serious. There was still the question of a possible shamming.
Kentridge	Did you think the plantar reflex could be feigned?
Lang	No.
Kentridge	Did you think a man could feign red blood cells in his cerebral spinal fluid?
Lang	No.
Kentridge	In terms of the Hippocratic Oath are not the interests of your patients paramount?
Lang	Yes.
Kentridge	But in this instance they were subordinated to the interests of security?
Lang	Yes.
Van Rooyen	If yesterday it was put to you Biko had only complained about a headache and back pains, that these were his only answers, and you said yes, that would have been wrong. It now appears also that he complained about his limbs and asked for a glass of water?
Lang	Yes.
Kentridge	This witness said with the utmost clarity that Biko was asked and answered only one question.
Van Rooyen	Is it possible for a person with medical knowledge to simulate in a plantar test a movement curve of the toes upwards instead of inwards?
Lang	I would say it was possible but I do not know of anybody who has done it. It is not a particularly easy reflex to read and it sometimes has to be repeated.
Gordon	Have you ever read about it?
Lang	No, but I have heard of a case.
Gordon	Can you tell us about it?
Lang	It involved another witness.
Gordon	It will be rather unique if a person can give you a positive extensor reflex. Did you make notes?

Lang	No, I did not make notes. I would rather like to change my answer to that. I have no knowledge about it.

This tantalising exchange went no further, but it left the extraordinary impression that Lang and someone else involved in the case set out to experiment whether or not a positive plantar reflex could be deliberately simulated.

Witness: Dr. Hersch

Van Rooyen	Nowhere in your report after you knew he had died did you say that you came to a definite conclusion that there was an organic condition.
Hersch	No, I did not, but one should have said it.
Van Rooyen	You did not say so in your report?
Hersch	Because I thought it was self-explanatory. It was not a good report. I had a conversation with Mr. Keeley before I was in contact with Dr. Lang. I had no further knowledge of the developments until I heard Biko had died.
Van Rooyen	You did not gain the impression that something serious was wrong?
Hersch	No, it was serious but not an emergency.
Van Rooyen	In your conversation with Mr. Keeley did you suggest brain damage and did Mr. Keeley accept it?
Hersch	Yes, he accepted the findings. He agreed there was brain damage.
Kentridge	Biko was not taken to a proper hospital.
Hersch	This was not in our hands. There is no doubt that had he been a private patient he would have been in hospital.
Kentridge	Would you have allowed Biko to go to Pretoria in a Land Rover on four cell mats?

Dr. Hersch replied that he would not have been unhappy if Mr. Biko's condition was the same as on examination.

Kentridge	If he had collapsed and was in a semi-coma?
Hersch	I would never have allowed a patient to go 700 miles by road in this condition.

Witness: Dr. B. Tucker

Dr. Tucker, on the other hand, had breathed a sigh of relief when he had heard that Biko was being taken to Pretoria where he would be under the observation of professional people.

von Lieres	Was Biko given all the care he needed?
Tucker	I would say the care he received was adequate.
Gordon	Why didn't you bring your influence to bear upon the authorities to ensure that he was transported by an ambulance, not a Land Rover?

Tucker	Col. Goosen assured me that he would be transported in as comfortable a manner as possible, in a Kombi on mattresses.
Gordon	Didn't it occur to you there might well have been an ethical responsibility to argue that if he could not go by air he should have gone by ambulance?
Tucker	That is correct. I thought that the mode of transport would amount to that of a quasi-ambulance.
Prins	Mr. Biko was transported with four cell mats and a number of blankets. Did you think it would be a shock absorbing bed?
Tucker	To a certain extent. A Kombi is far more comfortable to sit and lie in than a Land Rover.

Dr. Tucker was later recalled and questioned about the events following Biko's death, when the internal police examination was taking place.

Kentridge asked why Dr. Tucker had only made his affidavit on 19 October. Tucker said he was away on leave and when he had returned to Port Elizabeth he was told by Col. Goosen an affidavit was required. His second affidavit was made at the request of Major-General J. F. Kleinhaus, the investigating officer.

Tucker said Gen. Kleinhaus asked whether he had seen any abrasions and whether Biko had mentioned an assault; he also asked him whether he had been informed by Col. Goosen of what had occurred in Room 619 before the first medical examination.

Kentridge	General Kleinhaus simply asked you whether Col. Goosen had told you Biko had been aggressive and attacked a number of his staff?

Dr. Tucker confirmed this.

Kentridge	So Gen. Kleinhaus put words into your mouth?
Tucker	He asked questions and I answered them.
Kentridge	It seems a very strange sort of investigation by an investigating officer to do it this way.

Tucker told the Court that he spent about three hours with Gen. Kleinhaus and that Col. Goosen was present at the interview. 'He just listened', he said.

Kentridge	This three hour interview comes out in half a page in your affidavit.

Tucker said there had been a discussion of the photographs taken of Biko and that this had been the first time they had been able to read the report of the post-mortem examination.

Kentridge	Were you in Port Elizabeth on 13 September—the day after Biko died?
Tucker	I was.
Kentridge	Did no police officer come down at that stage and ask you about the case while the trail was still hot?
Tucker	No.

Dr. Tucker said his first consultation with counsel or an attorney took place in Port Elizabeth on 10 November.

96

Asked by Mr. Kentridge who the lawyer was, Dr. Tucker replied: Mr. Van Rooyen.

Kentridge   Mr. Van Rooyen, counsel for the police ? Do you mean the counsel for the police ?

Dr. Tucker confirmed it was the same person. Dr. Lang and Dr. Hersch had been present at the consultation but Col. Goosen was not there.

The Court heard that the week preceding the inquest another advocate, Mr. Pickard, had been called in to act as counsel for the doctors.

Thus the doctors' evidence concluded. None, on their own admission, had attempted to give or obtain for Biko any form of medical treatment.

X

Counsel's Submission on behalf of the Biko Family

These are the indisputed facts concerning the treatment of Mr. Biko.

Mr. Biko was detained on 18 August, 1977, whilst in good health. He died 26 days later. What the security police themselves admit they subjected him to during this period is more than a matter for comment. The admitted assaults on his dignity under the direction of Colonel Goosen are evidence of a callous disregard for his legal and human rights and are highly relevant in assessing the evidence of those who abused him:

He was left in solitary confinement from 19 August to 6 September. He was deprived even of the negligible rights he had as a section 6 detainee. His clothes were removed and he was left naked in his cell; he was not taken out for the minimum period of exercise in the open air; he was not allowed to purchase any food; he was not allowed proper washing facilities. His complaints to the magistrate on 2nd September did not even come to the notice of those against whom they were made.

He was brought to the interrogation room on the morning of 6 September 1977. At night he was handcuffed, and shackled by leg irons on his feet which in turn were locked on to walls. This was the position that he was expected to sleep in. He remained so shackled even after Colonel Goosen (according to his own evidence) suspected that he had suffered a stroke, and even after his hands, feet and ankles were swollen and cut.

He remained shackled on the mat after he was seen by Dr. Lang, for the whole day of the 7th and during the night of the 7th/8th and during the morning of the 8th. Security policemen say that he had not made use of toilet facilities offered, but the fact is that he was found in urine-wet trousers and blankets, on a wet mat, and was left there, shackled, until he was removed to the prison hospital at about 21.00h.

No channels of communication were established to report his condition to the doctors.

For contradictory and inadequate reasons he was moved from the prison hospital to a police cell, ostensibly to make it easier for Dr. Lang to see him regularly. In fact, this meant that he was removed from even the semi-skilled care of the prison warders; removed from a bed to a mat, and again left naked.

In a few hours he was found in a state of collapse on the floor. The senior officers and Dr. Tucker were again hurriedly called in. Again there was insistence on only a prison hospital, even if it was 1,200 km away, and even if only a van was available as transport.

He was transported approximately 1,200 kilometres lying naked in the back of a Landrover without any medically qualified person and with nothing more than a bottle of water by way of equipment.

No medical reports were furnished by the doctors of Port Elizabeth, nor were they asked for by the security policemen who took him to Pretoria.

Although he had to be carried into prison by four men using a mat as a stretcher, a further attempt was made by the security policemen from Port Elizabeth to persuade officials at the Pretoria Prison that he might be feigning illness, and that he was on a hunger strike.

He was sent all the way to Pretoria Prison because there, according to Colonel Goosen, there were 'outstanding medical facilities'. For Biko these facilities proved to be a mat in the corner of the cell, the attendance of a newly-qualified G.P. six hours after his arrival at the prison, a diagnosis based on false reports of a hunger strike, a drip and a vitamin injection, and nothing more.

At no time was any member of Biko's family or any friend informed of his condition. He died a miserable and lonely death on a mat on a stone floor in a prison cell.

It is difficult to comment on these facts in measured terms. Certainly Colonel Goosen's statement made after his death that everything was done for the comfort and health of Steve Biko is as cynical a statement as any heard in a court of law. Colonel Goosen, Major Snyman, Captain Siebert, Lieutenant Wilken, Dr. Lang and Dr. Tucker are all to a greater or lesser extent involved in the sorry treatment of Mr. Biko. Their alleged concern must be judged in the light of their conduct rather than their professions. The evidence of some of the security police of their tenderness towards those in their care becomes unacceptable in the light of this conduct and their use of improper methods of interrogation.

The Pathological Evidence — The Brain Injury

By the pathological evidence, the brain injury is dated as 4 to 8 days old by Prof. Loubser, Dr. Gluckman and Prof. Simpson—probably 5 to 6 days old; as probably 5 to 8 days old by Prof. Proctor; while Prof. Loubser and Prof. Simpson thought the injuries to the brain were nearer 5 than 12 days old.

The head injury was therefore suffered before the night of the 8 September, and not earlier than 4 or 5 September.

The Police Evidence is that Biko left Walmer at 10 a.m. on 6 September. He was fit and well. He then underwent seven or more hours of interrogation during which, according to his interrogators, he was in possession of all his faculties. This session ended at 6 p.m. At 7.30 a.m. on 7 September he was found by Colonel Goosen to be incoherent. He was not responding to stimuli, and Colonel Goosen spoke in terms of a 'stroke'.

The Clinical Evidence is that by 10 p.m. on the 8th Dr. Hersch had found unmistakable evidence of brain damage—(the extensor plantar reflex, echolalia and left-sided weakness).

Earlier on the same day Dr. Tucker's examination revealed neurological abnormalities (whether or not he realised it at the time):

Biko moved his left arm with difficulty; its reflexes were reduced. There was a doubtful up-going toe on the right side; he had difficulty in using his left leg; eneurisis had occurred.

These features reflected a neurological disorder.

At 9.30 on 7 September Dr. Lang, (whether or not he realised their significance) noted neurological abnormality:

Slurred or thick speech; the 'ataxic type' gait; a difference between the reflexes in Biko's arms.

This evidence places it beyond reasonable doubt that Mr. Biko had suffered his brain injury by 7.30 a.m. on the 7th. It also points to the very strong probability that the injury had been suffered not earlier than the night of the 6th. Note Colonel Goosen's telex which speaks of the fact that injuries were 'inflicted' at 7 a.m. on the 7th.

In the course of cross-examination we put it that Biko had been 'smashed up'. Police witnesses and district surgeons maintained that he showed no sign of this, that all they saw was a cut lip, a bruise on the chest and abrasions on wrists and ankles. This evades the real point of the indisputable evidence. On the morning of the 6 September Biko went into the interrogation room alive and well. At 7.30 a.m. on 7 September he was a physical and mental wreck.

It is clear, therefore, that Mr. Biko suffered his injuries either while in the custody of the night squad (Lieutenant Wilken, W/O Fouche and Coetzee) or the day squad (Major Snyman, Captain Siebert, W/O Marx, W/O Beneke, Sgt. Nieuwoudt). Nobody else can have direct knowledge of how he sustained his injuries. It is, therefore, for them to explain acceptably how he came to sustain them. In the absence of an acceptable explanation the court is entitled to draw an inference that one or more of them was responsible for unlawfully assaulting him.

If, in addition to failing to give an acceptable explanation, a false explanation is given, the inference of guilt is strengthened.

In this case it is submitted that no satisfactory explanation of the injuries has been given; and that false evidence of the events of 6 and 7 September has been given by members of the security branch.

No Satisfactory Explanation

From the Night Squad, Lieutenant Wilken and W/O Fouche, one has had a bare denial that Biko was assaulted. He was within their sight or their hearing at all times during the night. Both stated that any sound above a whisper could be heard by them. Nobody appears to have heard anything unusual. The affidavit of W/O Coetzee is similarly negative.

No explanation is to be found in this evidence.

From the Day Squad, all five members have given an account either orally or by affidavit. Their version consists of a story of aggression by Biko—for which false and conflicting explanations were given—followed by a struggle. It is said that the struggle was a violent one, that five men were needed to overpower him and that he went on struggling even after he was manacled. In the course of this struggling, it is said Biko and his captors bumped into the furniture and perhaps into the walls and may have fallen to the ground.

Can this version explain the brain injury? It cannot for the following reasons:

In the first place not one of the five is prepared to say that he saw Biko strike his forehead. Nor does anybody admit to having seen what would have been a fresh injury on his forehead—notwithstanding the fact that they saw the lip injury. Moreover—nobody mentioned either in his original affidavit or in his later statement to General Kleinhaus that Biko had or might have bumped his head.

In the statements taken by General Kleinhaus the policemen concerned had their attention specifically drawn to the question of brain injury; and were asked if they could give any explanation of it. The fact that nobody mentioned that Biko had or may have bumped his head either on a wall or on the floor leads irresistibly to the inference that that did not happen.

Neither Major Snyman nor any of his officers has given satisfactory, or even intelligible accounts of any impact which might account for the injury.

Major Snyman in the occurrence book stated as a fact that Biko had fallen 'with his head against the wall and his body on the ground'. But when pressed by the Court it became clear that he had seen nothing of the sort. He was drawing 'on inference'.

Captain Siebert is equally vague and unconvincing. In his original affidavit, he said that during the struggle 'we' fell against tables, chairs and on the ground. But when the question was pertinently put to him by General Kleinhaus all he could say was that it was not 'impossible' that the injury could have been sustained on the 7th. He said nothing about any particular fall and nothing about Biko's head being knocked against the wall. When asked whether he had seen Biko fall with his head against the wall, he said No, that it was he, Siebert himself, who bumped into the wall.

Warrant Officer Beneke does not claim to have seen any impact or possible impact to Biko's head. Warrant Officer Marx conceded that he had never said in his evidence that Biko sustained any head injuries, nor did Major Snyman ever say anything of the sort to him.

Notwithstanding the absence of any convincing evidence that anyone saw Biko sustain an impact to his head it might be argued that in a confused struggle in a crowded room he might have sustained a blow on his forehead which nobody noticed at the time. This in itself is possible, although highly unlikely. But the 'struggle' was an explanation of the injuries is entirely eliminated by the powerful medical evidence on the subject of unconsciousness. There is strong, convincing and uncontroverted evidence that the brain injury which Biko suffered must have resulted in a substantial period of unconsciousness.

Professor Proctor stated 'I would say, as far as medically one can say it, that this patient must have been unconscious'. He estimated a period of unconsciousness of ten to twenty minutes. It could not have been momentary. And if all the brain lesions were caused by one blow, the period of unconsciousness would have been greater.

Professor Simpson agreed that it was almost inconceivable that there would not have been unconsciousness following these lesions to the brain.

Professor Loubser, stated that he had no reason to disagree that there must have been a period of unconsciousness of at least ten minutes—more likely fifteen to twenty, and possibly up to an hour.

When asked by the court whether he agreed that it was 'virtually inconceivable that there would not have been an appreciable period of unconsciousness', his answer was 'That is my personal view and I agree with that; but the alternative that he was not unconscious is a distinct possibility that I cannot rule out'.

In the light of all this evidence, it must be accepted not merely on the balance of probabilities but for all practical purposes that the injury sustained must have resulted in a period of unconsciousness.

The account given by the various officers completely excludes any possibility of unconsciousness. *It follows that the struggle as described cannot be taken to explain the injuries.* Some other explanation is necessary but has not been forthcoming.

The possibility of a self-inflicted injury was mentioned in passing but not seriously mooted. None of the doctors appears ever to have come across the phenomenon of a self-inflicted brain injury, or to have read of it.

Even if it is medically not an impossibility, it is so improbable as not to be worth mention. During the time in question Mr. Biko was constantly under surveillance. None of the night squad heard or saw anything untoward; none of them suggests that Biko was ever out of his bed. As Professor Loubser says, to inflict that degree of injury himself, he would have had to bang his head against the wall with some considerable force 'and repetitively'.

The Furnishing of False Explanations

It is submitted that the police account of what took place on the morning of the 7th is untruthful. An analysis of the evidence shows that at some time in the night or the early hours of the 7th, possibly at 7.00 a.m., possibly earlier, injuries were inflicted on Mr. Biko. It must have been seen that he was unconscious; and his lack of reaction to stimuli as he began to come round caused concern to Colonel Goosen. The seriousness of the injuries was no doubt not realised, but it was nonetheless felt necessary to call in a doctor. Some of the injuries, such as the cut lip, could not be disguised. It was therefore necessary from the outset to give some explanation of his injuries which would make him out to be the aggressor, and justify any force used against him. The telex, concealed by Colonel Goosen as long as he was able to, and produced in this court at a late stage, throws a great deal of light on this. The telex speaks of injuries *inflicted* on Mr. Biko at 7.00 a.m. Colonel Goosen, in answer to his own counsel, said that he was referring to the minor injuries such as the lip injury. This cannot be true. The vital point in the telex was that Mr. Biko's inability to speak was directly related to the injuries inflicted. No one could have believed that a mere injury to the lip would have accounted for his failure to react, his incoherence, or the symptoms generally which Colonel Goosen chose to describe as evidence possibly of a 'stroke'.

Notwithstanding what he could see for himself, Dr. Lang was induced to give a clean certificate, one which he acknowledged in this court was substantially incorrect and which we submit was plainly false.

With the certificate for protection in case the detainee should later complain, no further steps were taken by Colonel Goosen. However, when Biko again manifested alarming symptoms on the night of the 7th, further action became necessary. That action was the making of Major Snyman's entry in the occurrence book. There a foundation was laid for a version which would explain Biko's injury as caused by 'falling with his head against the wall'. The explanations given for this *late* entry have been contradictory and unacceptable. In his main affidavit, Major Snyman gave as his reason that Biko was still 'stubbornly' refusing to react to questions. In his evidence he gave as reason that Biko was shamming—a ridiculous reason. Colonel Goosen said in evidence that the entry was made because of an injury to W/O Beneke. And in the telex, the reason for not making the entry at the proper time is said to be the existence of Dr. Lang's certificate.

It is instructive to compare the telex dated 16 September with Colonel Goosen's affidavit dated 17 September. The telex clearly connects Biko's refusal to speak with the injuries. The affidavit does not; on the contrary, the detainee's condition is attributed to a suspected stroke. The telex, intended only for the eyes of the security police, says nothing about any suspicion of shamming. The affidavit, intended for other eyes, is at pains to introduce the alleged suspicion of shamming—the refrain taken up by all the Security Police officers when compelled by circumstances to give some explanation. It is little wonder that Colonel Goosen denied the existence of any telex messages.

This false denial shows that he was well aware of the contradictions between what was stated in the telex and what he had said in his affidavits and evidence. Why else should he have lied?

At that stage when they were giving evidence, and it was their case that the brain injuries were probably sustained in the 'scuffle', both Colonel Goosen and Major Snyman were impelled to say that they always had it in mind that Biko's mysterious state might be attributable to a head injury. But this is the one possibility that was never mentioned by Colonel Goosen or anyone else to Dr. Lang,

Dr. Tucker or Dr. Hersch. What can be the explanation for that? I suggest only a desire to conceal the true circumstances in which the injuries were received.

Consider also the fact that amid the host of irrelevant photographs of places 'pointed out' to the police photographer, the one thing that was never pointed out was any place where Biko might have bumped his head in the struggle.

Major Snyman's statement that he demonstrated to General Kleinhaus how the alleged fall of Biko against the wall took place is obviously unacceptable; there is no mention of this in any of the affidavits which the General took and it is inconceivable that even in the type of investigation carried out by the General, this point would not have been noted by him.

It is fairly easy to make up a general story of a 'scuffle' in which anything may happen including the bumping of a head against a wall or the floor; but it is not easy for the police officers to explain why this possibility which looms so large in their present evidence played no part in their reports to the doctors or in their attitude to Biko. If they really believed that he had, without fault on the part of the police, possibly sustained a head injury in the struggle, it is inconceivable that they could have clung so firmly to the idea that he was shamming. There are furthermore numerous points on which the police evidence concerning the origin of Mr. Biko's alleged 'aggression' is demonstrably false.

First and most important is Major Snyman's attempted explanation of why Biko should have 'gone berserk'.

Major Snyman begins a circumstantial account of the *facts* with which he confronted the detainee on the morning of the 7th. He denied that these 'facts' were simply plucked out of the air, and said himself (without prompting from his counsel) that they already had sworn statements in that connection and counsel then tendered the sworn statements to the Court. It was made clear that the sworn statements handed in were the sworn statements with which Biko was confronted. Major Snyman was specifically asked whether he had put these sworn statements to the detainee on the morning of the 7th and he confirmed this.

It was then shown that the sworn statements were dated after Biko's death. After this ignominious retreat, Snyman made some attempt to suggest that he had in mind unsworn statements. But the other police officers admitted that on the morning of the 7th no documents at all were put to Mr. Biko.

Consequently, what we have is a clear and plain case of deliberate perjury on the part of Major Snyman. What object could he have had in putting forward a false reason for Mr. Biko's alleged outburst, other than to conceal something to his own discredit?

Major Snyman's careful story of the confrontation of Biko with the facts is entirely contradicted by the affidavits made last September when the full implications of the case were not yet clear to the police officers. Major Snyman, in his affidavit, says nothing about confronting Biko with facts; he speaks of questions to which Biko would not respond. Captain Siebert, in his affidavit, says that Major Snyman was putting questions to Biko which Biko was answering in a hostile manner. Warrant Officer Marx suggests that Biko's outburst started only after twenty minutes of interrogation. Warrant Officer Beneke also indicates that there was about fifteen minutes questioning before the alleged incident.

Captain Siebert's further attempt to decorate the story by describing how Biko was shocked by the confrontation, and how he went 'ashen grey' is a most unconvincing afterthought; in his affidavit there is no mention of this, and Biko is said to have been answering in a hostile manner right up to the moment when he sprang up.

Indeed the whole story of the alleged confession in the late afternoon of the 6th is unacceptable.

There are indications in the evidence that this confession was a fabrication. First, Lieutenant Wilken's statement to Mr. Biko that he should 'stop wasting people's time and tell the truth' would hardly be comprehensible if Biko had already confessed. And finally the fact, stated by Brigadier Zietsman in affidavit, that when Colonel Goosen was asked how far the investigation had progressed, he made no mention of Biko's confession. On the contrary, all that he reported was Lieutenant Wilken's report of Biko's request for fifteen minutes and his subsequent *failure* to make a statement.

From the time of Dr. Lang's first visit on the 7th, right up to the last days' evidence in this court, the police officers have repeatedly stated that they believed that Mr. Biko was shamming. They pressed this view on the doctors; and they still maintain that this was their genuine belief. This is also demonstrably untrue.

Colonel Goosen, in his evidence, based his belief on gossip that Biko in a previous detention had shown 'similar symptoms', whatever that may mean. This is what he said to the Port Elizabeth doctors. But no attempt was made to substantiate this. It was not confirmed by any other officer.

As to the cause or likely cause of death there can be no doubt whatsoever. On the evidence of Professors Loubser, Proctor and Simpson and Dr. Gluckman it has been established that Mr. Biko died as a result of at least three brain lesions caused by the external application of force to his head. The suggestions made in the affidavits of certain police officers and highly placed persons outside court, that Mr. Biko was on a hunger strike, or that he had become dehydrated or that he had suffered a stroke or that he suffered from kidney disease, need no serious consideration.

The other question which the court has to answer is whether the death was brought about by any act or omission involving or amounting to an offence on the part of any person. The Court may find that a person is responsible, and if his identity has been disclosed in the evidence the court should name him. The fact that the identity of a wrongdoer has not been disclosed in the evidence does not, however, mean that the court is entitled to make a finding that no person is guilty of any act or omission causing the death. A negative finding would be tantamount to exonerating all the persons involved in the handling of Mr. Biko. A conclusion which would have the effect of exonerating all concerned is one that cannot on the evidence as a whole, be reached by any reasonable man.

Our submission is that one or more of the security policemen is responsible for the injury which caused Steven Biko's death; and that the probabilities are that the injuries were inflicted deliberately, unlawfully, without good cause. Those responsible are accordingly guilty of at least the crime of culpable homicide.

We do not submit that Mr. Biko was *wilfully* killed in the sense that whoever assaulted him wanted him to die. We submit that he was beaten; and the person or people who did this did not at the time care whether he was seriously injured or not.

This court's function is not to try the security policemen nor to convict them. An inquest is not a criminal trial at the instance of the Attorney General nor indeed is it a private prosecution with the representatives of the family as the prosecutors. The function of the court at an inquest is an attempt to ascertain whether or not there is evidence that, on all the probabilities, establishes at least a *prima facie* case that some person, known or unknown, is responsible for the death of the deceased. The court, therefore, does not have to come to a verdict beyond any reasonable doubt. The court must express an opinion as to whether or not there is a *prima facie* case. Whatever the court's view may be in relation to a *prima facie* case, if it is apparent that further investigations should be conducted, it is the court's duty to point this out to the Attorney-General, in the hope that the further investigation will take place.

Although the Court's finding is not a final one, it is nevertheless an important one, in which the members of the family have a real and substantial interest.

We as representatives of the family are entitled to avail and have availed ourselves of the opportunity to place information before the court and to cross-examine witnesses in order to assist the court in coming to the correct conclusion.

However, we have been subject to a number of limitations. We have no right to subpoena witnesses. Nor in the nature of things could we produce an eye-witness to the treatment received by Biko in Sanlam Buildings. What we have tried to do is to test and probe the evidence made available to us by the court. We have been permitted full scope by the court in cross-examining the witnesses called, although we would, of course have liked to cross-examine other persons too whom the court felt it unnecessary to call.

In the task of probing and testing the evidence of the police officers and the witnesses, we had the assistance of the court, but none of the other counsel in court. All, including the Deputy-Attorney-General, appeared to us to ask no question but to repair or extenuate the effect of our cross-examination. Notwithstanding public promises of the fullest investigation, the investigation undertaken by the police had peculiar and unfortunate limitations. First, it appears that the investigating officer made his appearance in Port Elizabeth only a month or more after Mr. Biko's death; yet the fact of Mr. Biko's injury—if not its cause—was ascertainable from Prof. Loubser by the morning of 13 September. The investigating officer took numerous affidavits, many in duplicated form, and all self-serving. He failed to search for or take possession of documents—not even the telex messages or the hospital bed letter. He made no search of the Security Branch's office, whether for possible blunt instruments or for anything else.

He seems to have made no effort to find out whether there was any truth in the rumour spread by Col. Goosen that in previous detention Biko had shown 'similar symptoms'; nor does he seem to have subjected Col. Goosen to any real interrogation on this or any other subject. A police investigation would require far more spirit and initiative than asking suspects to fill in a form or answer a few simple questions. Accordingly we must base our submissions on the probabilities which arise from the medical evidence, the circumstances surrounding Mr. Biko's death, and the evidence, often unwilling and evasive, of the police officers and doctors concerned.

Our submission in simple summary is that Mr. Biko was assaulted and that is how his brain lesions were caused. The security police deny that he was assaulted and now appear to suggest that his injury may have been accidentally caused in an incident on the morning of the 7th, in which Mr. Biko was said to be the aggressor. We assume that the fanciful theories of Colonel Goosen that the injuries were self-inflicted in attempts to commit suicide are not going to be persisted in. The main issue before the court, therefore, is whether, considering the evidence, there is reason to conclude that one or other of the security policemen assaulted Biko while he was in their custody.

There is no direct evidence that any particular security policeman assaulted Biko. The reason for the absence of such direct evidence or eye-witness evidence is due to the fact that some at least of the security police have entered into a conspiracy of silence as to what really happened.

However, in order to reach the conclusion that Biko was assaulted, it is not necessary to have direct evidence. Circumstantial evidence may be far more cogent than direct evidence.

The circumstantial evidence which shows that one or more of the policemen assaulted Mr. Biko during the night of the 6th/7th or the morning of 7 September falls broadly into the following categories:

The time when the injuries were sustained, namely between the evening of the 6th and 7.30 a.m. on 7 September.

The failure of the police officers to give any truthful or acceptable explanation of the circumstances in which Mr. Biko received his injuries; they concealed the truth, and in this court some of them at least have given demonstrably false evidence.

The behaviour of certain of the doctors and their failure to see what must of necessity have been visible to them, which shows that they too were drawn into the conspiracy of silence.

The callous treatment of Mr. Biko by the security police.

The overwhelming balance of probabilities on the medical evidence that the 'scuffle' on the morning of the 7th could not have caused the brain injuries found post mortem. This story bears all the hallmarks of invention.

It has already been pointed out that the telex makes no mention of shamming. Certainly after Dr. Hersch's examination none of the officers could honestly have believed that Biko was shamming, yet they persisted with their story. Colonel Goosen's second affidavit, of Biko's first feigning weakness in one arm and then in another was shown to be false—none of the doctors would support it. And the clinical findings of Dr. Tucker and Dr. Hersch show that the complaint in both cases was in respect of the left arm—another pure invention by Colonel Goosen.

It is not possible to believe that Colonel Goosen made the urgent arrangements which he did on Sunday evening, the 11th, for someone whom he honestly believed to be a malingerer.

He says there that at the time Biko was sent to Pretoria he still had no reason to believe that the man was sick. This is the man whom in his own telex he described as being in a 'semi-coma'. There are other false statements on this topic scattered through Colonel Goosen's evidence. For example, his affidavit that he was assured by all the doctors (including Dr. Hersch) that there was nothing physically wrong with Biko; and that it was the 'general opinion' that the detainee was shamming. This was plainly untrue; his attempted explanation of the words 'general opinion' show this witness at his most shifty.

Colonel Goosen attempted to deny that the suggestion of shamming came from him to the doctors. He suggested that it was the doctors who conveyed the suggestion to him. This is plainly false. Perhaps the most absurd and flagrant example of Colonel Goosen's prevarication is the 'theory' in his second affidavit. Even at that stage he put up the theory that Biko's head injury had been *self-inflicted* on the early morning of the 9th. (i.e. *after* Dr. Hersch's clear findings of evidence of neurological damage). He maintained in evidence, that when he made that affidavit, he still thought that Biko had been shamming on the 7th and the 8th—in other words that on the 7th and 8th Biko was shamming the effects of a injury which he actually suffered on the 9th.

No honest man could have believed the theories stated in his affidavit. They constituted an attempt to draw attention *away* from the fact that the head injuries had actually been suffered not later than the early morning of the 7th, and in circumstances to which Colonel Goosen did not dare honestly to advert.

Colonel Goosen's attitude is reflected in that of other members of his branch. For example, Captain Siebert, Lieutenant Wilken and Warrant Officer Fouche were all responsible for taking Mr. Biko in a semi coma from Port Elizabeth to Pretoria. They had to carry him to the van. He was plainly comatose during the journey. He had to be carried into the prison in Pretoria. At Pretoria Prison, when Sergeant Pretorius said he was afraid for Biko's life, the reaction of Captain Siebert and Lieutenant Wilken was to suggest that he was still shamming.

In this court they maintained that position.

Warrant Officer Fouche, without being able to give any credible reason for it, echoed this view when giving evidence on the last day of the hearing.

There is also the unexplained mystery of the alleged hunger strike. What is known is that the Ministerial head of Colonel Goosen's department very shortly after Mr. Biko's death issued statements in which it was said that on 5 September he had threatened a hunger strike and refused to speak. What is abundantly clear is that Biko did not 'threaten' a hunger strike and particularly that he did not do so on 5 September. The question remains how it was that statements, which were false and misleading, could be made and repeated at the highest level. And why was it that in the official statements there was no mention of this 'scuffle' which has now taken on such importance in the police evidence? Who was responsible for this misleading statement? And, equally important, who was responsible for the fact that although published amidst a public outcry, it was never corrected? The Security Police have not seen fit to clear up this mystery; nor has the Minister of Police. Although Colonel Goosen has denied that it started with him, there can be little doubt that it must have originated in the Port Elizabeth office.

A further unexplained mystery, which casts doubt on the truthfulness of the police officers, is their concerted denial of having seen the obvious injury on Mr. Biko's forehead. As Professor Loubser and Dr. Gluckman indicated, it is hardly credible that this would not have been seen by any of the police officers. The doctors did not admit having seen it either—a fact which will be discussed when *their* evidence is considered in detail.

The inference from the false evidence of the Police Officers

It is necessary to consider the effect of this mass of false evidence. Sometimes a false statement does no more than destroy the credibility of the man who makes it. But in many cases the making of a false statement is in itself a piece of positive evidence.

This is particularly so when the obvious inference from a piece of false evidence is that there is something which the witness wishes to hide. This is plainly such a case. There could be no reason for the mass of false evidence referred to above (and it is by no means a complete recital of all the falsehoods in the police evidence), unless there was some circumstance connected with Mr. Biko's injuries which the police wanted to hide. No other explanation can reasonably suggest itself.

The false evidence is of a piece with the actual conduct of the police at the time. They constantly distracted attention from the possibility of a head injury and pressed the theory of shamming. They kept the detainee in Sanlam building as long as they could, and persistently refused to allow him to go into a Provincial Hospital. They gave instructions when he went to Port Elizabeth Prison that no black member of the police force should come into contact with him.

They gave a false name when sending the samples to the Institute of Medical Research and his true name was kept at least from Mr. Keeley and possibly from Dr. Hersch.

They were anxious to get him out of Port Elizabeth Hospital and back into the Walmer police cells as soon as possible; and they preferred to send him by road to Pretoria rather than put him in a Port Elizabeth hospital.

The falsehoods with which we are dealing are not on peripheral or collateral matters. In the words of Judge Schreiner (R. *v.* Gani, 1958), what is before the court is not merely a story put forward by an untrustworthy witness, 'it is the story of which the central, justificatory feature must be rejected as a concoction'.

The only inference which can properly be drawn is one of guilt.

The Port Elizabeth Doctors' Findings

The medical profession's general reputation has led courts in the past, whenever an issue arose as to whether a prisoner seen by a doctor had been assaulted or not, to place great if not absolute reliance on the district surgeon's findings. We are compelled to submit that in this case the proved facts show that not only can the court *not* rely on the evidence of Drs. Ivor Lang and Benjamin Tucker, but that an analysis of the evidence shows that they joined with the security police in this conspiracy of silence. Not only can the court *not* rely on their evidence that they saw no injury, other than the lip injury, and that no complaints were made to them by Mr. Biko; but their admitted lack of enquiry about the possible cause of his injuries and/or the probable cause of the suspected brain damage shows clearly that, at the very best, they turned a blind eye. Dr. Hersch is not specifically included in these criticisms, even though his stated failure to see the injury on Mr. Biko's left temple and eye is difficult to accept.

Dr. Ivor Lang cannot be believed for the following reasons: He was not able to explain the reason why he issued the certificate; why the complaint that he noted on the certificate was other than that made by Colonel Goosen; why he had not noted the injury on the lip, the ankles, the wrists, the swelling of the hands and feet nor the bruises over the sternum. His concession that the certificate was 'highly inaccurate' and his statement that he did not know why Colonel Goosen may have wanted it are sufficient grounds to disbelieve him on any of the matters where his evidence has been put in issue.

In leading questions put by counsel for the security police, an attempt was made to rehabilitate Dr. Lang on this point. However, Dr. Lang's acceptance that he only issued the certificate in the form he did at the specific request of Colonel Goosen in order that Goosen's records may be kept 'straight', may be evidence of a degree of subservience which goes a long way to prove the submission being made.

This purported explanation is in conflict with Dr. Lang's statement earlier, that he could not answer nor explain why the additional matters were not put into his certificate.

Dr. Lang's inability to answer the question why he did not ask Mr. Biko about his injuries, when he himself says that he suspected a head injury when he saw the lip, is inexcusable from a professional man on whom a grave responsibility has been placed to protect helpless people in detention. What value can be placed on the evidence of a district surgeon who says that the reason why he did not ask an injured person how he got his injuries, was because he assumed that the patient would have told him? In the presence of a colonel, or whilst lying in an interrogation room in the immediate vicinity of his interrogators!

In answer to Counsel for the Police, Dr. Lang said Mr. Biko had ample opportunity to complain to him. His report was misleading in giving lack of co-operation as reason for the ataxic gait, when in evidence he says that he attributed it to the swelling of the feet.

He failed to note in his report that he found Mr. Biko shackled, and only mentioned this for the first time in his affidavit of 20 October.

His decision to remove Mr. Biko from the prison hospital to the Walmer Police Station is inexplicable, if one has regard to Mr. Keeley's affidavit and the cursory enquiries made by him of prison officials.

His evidence in relation to his conversation with Mr. Keeley is in conflict with the affidavit of Mr. Keeley. The probabilities clearly favour Mr. Keeley's version.

His statement to Biko at the prison that there was 'not much wrong with him'; his entry on the bed letter that no pathology could be found, and his explanations for these statements clearly show that he is not speaking the truth, even if he merely describes them as 'incorrect'.

His failure to enquire from Biko and/or Goosen whether there may not have been a head injury is not explained in cross examination or in answer to the Court.

His failure to see the head injury (having regard to the fact that he saw Mr. Biko on the 7th, twice on the 8th, the 9th and the 10th) cannot be explained, except on the basis that he did not examine properly, or that Dr. Lang has made himself a party to the conspiracy of silence initiated by Colonel Goosen and his officers.

Dr. Lang himself offers no satisfactory explanation. His reliance upon hearsay evidence of Mr. Biko's condition at the prison hospital, which induced him to move him to the police cells so that he may more closely observe him and then failed to do so, shows a lack of responsibility towards his patient so extraordinary for a doctor that the most adverse inference must be drawn against Dr. Lang's credibility.

His reliance upon information given by untrained persons in coming to a conclusion that Biko's condition had improved on the Friday when it in fact had deteriorated further, strengthens the submission being made.

Dr. Lang's denial that Mr. Biko was 'smashed up' cannot be of any assistance to anyone wanting to submit that he was not; a minimum of three lesions in the brain, two injuries on the lip and injury on the chest, abrasions on the wrists and ankles and swollen hands and feet, most of which Dr. Lang missed may not in the minds of many be construed as an exaggeration if described as 'smashed up'.

Dr. Lang's unreliability and how easily he is influenced is best illustrated by his uncritical acceptance of whatever was put to him in cross examination by Counsel for the Police.

In view of the fact that he had consulted with Counsel for the Police (before giving evidence in Court), very little if any weight should be attached to his evidence when he readily concedes matters in favour of the Security Police.

His consultation with Counsel for the Police, at the offices of the Security Police, at a time when he knew that his patient had died, and when he must have realised that he had been misled about his condition, not only shows lack of sensitivity but a degree of identification between medical practitioner and the Security Police whose conduct he knew was about to be investigated.

Dr. Benjamin Tucker cannot be believed on matters on which his evidence has been put in issue for the following reasons: He too identified himself with the Security Police by attending the consultation held by their Counsel (before being called to give evidence).

Although he was called in by Colonel Goosen and told that Mr. Biko had not passed urine for a substantial period of time, he makes no searching enquiry when he finds his clothes and bedding wet with urine.

His persistence in making assumptions about the causes of the injuries on Mr. Biko which he admits he saw, is not in accordance with the practice of District Surgeons, far less of a Chief District Surgeon.

No satisfactory explanation was given for his omission in the report of the injuries to the ankles.

The superficial nature of the examination and/or the inaccuracy of the report is illustrated by his evidence that he only asked Mr. Biko one question; but he says in his report that Biko was mentally alert and answered questions in an indistinct manner.

His evidence that he asked no questions to test the memory of Mr. Biko when he had been told that he may have suffered a stroke, is inexplicable.

The finding recorded by him as 'lack of co-operation' was clearly wrong in view of the concession that sufficient evidence was found that there was organic disease.

His failure to enquire whether or not there was the possibility of a head injury once he had found the presence of a doubtful extensor plantar reflex, is clear evidence that he did not wish to ask questions which might embarrass the Security Police.

He evaded the questions of the cross examiner and the court in relation to his state of mind after his examination of the patient on the 8th, and more especially after the findings of Dr. Hersch.

The condition that Dr. Tucker says he found Mr. Biko in on Sunday 11th is at variance with the concern of Colonel Goosen and the bizarre behaviour noted by prison warders.

On his own evidence the examination on the 11th must have been a cursory one; and his authorising the removal of Mr. Biko by road from Port Elizabeth to Pretoria is consistent with a desire to please Colonel Goosen and possibly to rid himself of the responsibility.

His persistence 'despite Dr. Hersch's findings' that there was no organic disease, does not bear critical examination.

For a registered medical practitioner to say that there were no signs of organic disease if one ignored the positive plantar reflex and the level of consciousness is so absurd that one must seek some reason for such a statement.

He admits that his affidavit, though deliberately made, contained a vitally incorrect statement.

In common with all the security policemen and all those who were allowed to see Mr. Biko, Dr. Tucker failed to notice the obvious injury on Mr. Biko's temple.

His statement that he considered Biko's condition satisfactory, and that is why he gave leave for the patient to be transported to Pretoria, is further evidence of his desire to accommodate the Security Police. His answers on this issue are clearly incorrect when analysed in cross-examination and is directly contradicted by the telex, which described Mr. Biko's condition at the time in question as semi comatose.

The absence of inquiry from the orderly at the prison hospital or from Dr. Lang as to Mr. Biko's clinical picture from the evening of the 8th to the afternoon of the 11th is evidence of lack of concern for the patient.

Dr. Tucker's concession that (in a hypothetical example) he would have treated a non-detainee differently and have insisted on his hospitalisation, is further evidence that he had abrogated his responsibility as a doctor, and was guided by Colonel Goosen.

To a lesser extent criticisms may be levelled against Dr. Hersch for his failure to insist that Mr. Biko should have been hospitalised; his failure to react positively to the extensor plantar reflex; the apparent contradiction in the report on the spinal fluid; and above all his failure to enquire as to whether or not there had been a head injury. His failure to see the injury on Mr. Biko's temple is also inexplicable, as is the wrong name of the patient on the sample. His professed ignorance cannot be correct, as he would have had to tie up the sample with the report and the patient that he had seen.

The relationship of the District Surgeons to Colonel Goosen was one of subservience, bordering on collusion. Their obvious neglect of their patient's interests, and their deference to the requirements of the security police was a breach of their professional duty, which may have contributed to the final result. They should not have tamely accepted Colonel Goosen's refusal in any circumstances to send Mr. Biko to a proper hospital.

Their conduct is of a piece with Colonel Goosen's disregard of the statutory regulations and orders by which he ought to have regulated his conduct. He did not regard himself as working under statute.

For whatever precise reason, the doctors felt themselves beholden to the security police. Upon being called in, Dr. Lang gave a patently false certificate.

113

Neither he, not his superior, Dr. Tucker, made any inquiry of their patient as to the origin of even the lip injury which, at least, they admit seeing. They did not even direct any inquiry to the police.

This studied lack of curiosity can only be explained either by their active collaboration with the police; or a deliberate election not to embarrass the police, nor indeed themselves, by asking questions to which the answers were obvious.

They—no doubt in common with the police—did not fear initially for Mr. Biko's life. On the contrary, it must have seemed that the course of time would heal Mr. Biko without their medical intervention, which would have had to be given in concert with officials of hospitals who would no doubt be more curious than they were.

And as time passed, one falsehood was compounded by another: Dr. Lang's false report to Biko that nothing wrong was found; and Dr. Tucker's claim that the dying man was in a satisfactory condition on his removal to Pretoria.

The police felt confident that they could rely upon the doctors to support them. And their confidence was justified. Perhaps strengthened thereby they, with gross impertinence, present to this court a totally implausible account of Mr. Biko's death, starting with a fanciful description of a struggle, violent in the extreme, in which no blow was struck; a bizarre account of an alleged shamming when to any candid observer a man's progress to his death was being seen and described; and all the while the refusal to acknowledge the head injury.

A court—including an inquest court—is the brake upon the abuse of power. It must be made known by this court that the penalty for falsehood contemptuously fabricated is not merely rebuke or reprimand but a firm finding adverse to the fabricators; if you create a tissue of lies it can only be that you dare not speak the truth.

Accordingly the verdict, which we submit is the only one reasonably open to this court, is one finding that the death of Mr. Biko was due to a criminal assault upon him by one or more of the eight members of the security police in whose custody he was at Sanlam Building on 6 or 7 September, 1977.

This inquest has exposed grave irregularity and misconduct in the treatment of a single detainee. It has incidentally revealed the dangers to life and liberty involved in the system of holding detainees incommunicado.

A firm and clear verdict may help to prevent further abuse of the system. In the light of disquieting evidence before this court, any verdict which can be seen as an exoneration of the Port Elizabeth security police will unfortunately be interpreted as a licence to abuse helpless people with impunity.

This court cannot allow that to happen.

114

XI

The Verdict

The Deputy Attorney General also made a closing submission, in which he stated that no one could be blamed for the death of Biko:

Von Lieres: The real inquiry at this inquest centres on whether the evidence points to an act or omission on the part of the police, doctors or prison officials, which led to the death of the deceased, Stephen Bantu Biko.

We have had evidence that the rubicon was crossed six to eight hours after the infliction of the injury, and we accept that the latest that the head injury could have been caused was approximately 7.30 on the morning of 7 September. On the evidence the deceased was therefore beyond help by about 3 o'clock on the afternoon of the 7th.

I submit on the evidence that neither doctors nor police could have known this and that his death was therefore not caused by any act or omission on their part, amounting to an offence.

Your Worship, this is a rather sad case and one which in my view once again highlights the fact that where one is concerned with two extreme opposites, the police on the one hand, and the detainee on the other, there is seldom ground to find what one could call common 'ground'. Literally, it seems to me as Rudyard Kipling said 'never the twain shall meet' . . .

Our respectful submission is that you will come to the conclusion that in this particular case there is no positive evidence that the deceased's death was caused by an act or omission of any person.

These words foreshadowed the findings. After 14 days of evidence and expert witnesses, Pretoria's Chief Magistrate closed the inquest into the death in detention of Stephen Biko with a finding that took 80 seconds to deliver in both official languages, English and Afrikaans. Reporters were still fumbling for their notebooks when he rose and the court was adjourned.

Mr. Marthinus Prins found: 'The cause or likely cause of Mr. Biko's death was a head injury, followed by extensive brain injury and other complications including renal failure.

'The head injury was probably sustained on the morning of 7 September during a scuffle with Security Police in Port Elizabeth. The available evidence does not prove that death was brought about by an act or omission involving an offence by any person'.

'*They killed Steve Biko*' was the chant taken up by crowds of Africans outside the courtroom after the verdict, and largely endorsed by the Western press. The London *Times* wrote:

'Nobody reading the reported evidence can draw any other conclusion but that the police are now an autonomous power in South Africa—strong enough to break rules, mislead or pressure ministers, overawe and compel the collusion of medical practitioners as well as committing and compounding perjury'.[29]

And a few days later: 'White South Africa has given a dusty answer for those who were so naive as to think United Nations sanctions would reduce Mr. Vorster's vote . . . The Biko inquest leads to no other reasonable conclusion than that he was illegally killed by the security forces and that, following this, the government responsible for those security forces has been returned with a larger majority. The white electorate cannot explain if it is inferred that they have this week consciously taken on themselves the guilt for what has been done to Biko and those like him. They have marked their foreheads as well as their ballot papers'.[30]

'The sheer perversity of the finding would cause dismay to all of black and some of white South Africa', wrote the *Guardian*. 'On Wednesday, when the National Party sailed back into power with a huge majority over liberal white opinion, Mr. Kruger himself beat his constituency opponent by ten to one . . . The verdicts of the electorate and the coroner cannot be kept separate. Both sanction a campaign of represssion against the black opposition, and discourage any interference in the conduct of it . . . (Mr. Prins) has presided over a judicial process which gave some semblance of respect for the law, but he has made an utter travesty of it . . . Present and future detainees now know what to expect'.[31]

'Now we are all accountable,' wrote the Johannesburg *Sunday Times*. 'The Biko inquest has served one or two useful purposes. It has exposed in chilling detail, how the system of detention operates . . . Nobody can plead ignorance. Nobody can say, But I didn't know . . . Every South African must now answer to his own conscience . . . and submit to the judgement of history on his actions'.[32] The paper went on to point out that the inquest had also vindicated the three Johannesburg newspapers whose accounts of Biko's injuries were confirmed in detail by the court, despite efforts by the Minister to silence and reprimand the press through the Press Council.

In an English language broadcast for abroad on 5 December, South African radio admitted that the death of Biko had disturbed many South Africans. 'As the Prime Minister, Mr. Vorster, has said, it was most unfortunate that Mr. Biko should have died'. The broadcast went on to praise the conduct of the inquest, held in an open court, demonstrating the openness of the South African legal system. And then to object, in anger, to the gross interference in South Africa's domestic affairs—from the United States in particular—following the verdict. 'The United States Government has no right to challenge directly a court verdict in South Africa or any other country with a free judicial system . . . To say that Mr. Biko's death resulted from a system which permits gross mistreatment in violation of the most basic human rights, is absurd . . . It would be nearer the truth (to say that he) was a victim of a confrontation in South Africa which had been recklessly supported from abroad, the victim, more

116

particularly, of instilling among black activists the notion that it is their right to rule all of South Africa—and to hell with the established order'.[33]

Was it worth it? asked South African journalist Roger Osmond, writing from Pretoria, and answered: Yes, it was. No one can any longer plead ignorance of Special Branch behaviour. 'We know now as we didn't know before that a detainee can be kept naked in a prison cell for three weeks, that he can be deprived of exercise, washing facilities and the right to buy food in direct contradiction of regulations, and that he can be kept handcuffed and in irons, chained to a grille for more than 48 hours. We know that he can be allowed to lie in his urine-soaked trousers on urine-soaked mats, while district surgeons don't even suggest a change of clothing, that doctors can miss classic symptoms of brain damage, that when the doctors eventually begin to worry they meekly follow Special Branch orders that he cannot be allowed anywhere near a decent hospital, that even when he is supposed to be under observation for brain damage he can be moved from a prison hospital back into a police cell, that a doctor can authorise a 700-mile journey overnight without first getting the results of a lumbar puncture, that the same doctor does not check whether the form of transport is the same as that promised by the Special Branch. We have also learned that a detainee can be sent naked on his last journey resting on prison mats with a blanket for a pillow, a couple of Special Branch men with no medical training as orderlies, a water container as the sole medicine, that when they reach Pretoria they persist in saying that the detainee is shamming, that no medical report accompanies the semi-comatose detainee, that a man hours away from death can be given a vitamin injection and a drip and that he can be allowed to die alone on a cell floor.

'And apart from Sydney Kentridge who, with his legal team, emerged as the heroes of the courtroom, nobody even bothers to comment on this chapter of inhumanity. Not Prins, not Kruger, not the unrepentant Special Branch. There is no word of sorrow or anger by the authorities, not even a suggestion detainees in future won't suffer the same treatment. They just don't care. And that is what South Africa voted for'.[34]

117

XII

Unanswered Questions

Despite limitations of method and purpose, the inquest had in some respects assumed the nature of a trial. The revelations of 'admitted assaults' on Biko's dignity and of a 'callous disregard for his legal and human rights' had proved so shocking that inevitable questions arose: why had the South African authorities permitted the inquest? Why had it allowed horrific details to be sent all over the world? And how did such apparent free judicial procedure within the court and freedom of expression through the press equate with general trends in South Africa, and with the final, cursory verdict? Superficially there appear to be contradictions.

And there were other questions that remained unanswered. These were:

● **The hunger strike.** What was the origin and purpose of this story? No answer came out of the inquest.

● **The naked man.** Conditions under which detainees are held are not normally revealed; it cannot be known with certainty whether or not other detainees have been kept naked. This was the first time such action became known. Was Biko's treatment special in this respect? Why was he kept naked?

● **The bath episode.** This bizarre incident was never explained. How did Biko twice get dressed and climb into a bath?

● **The journey to Pretoria.** Even taken at their face value, the reasons given by Goosen are absurd. Port Elizabeth is a large town with excellent hospitals. Why, then, this last desperate journey for the dying man?

● **The flaws in the police story.** This remains the most important question and was not answered satisfactorily at the end of the inquest. Why, in view of the fact that nobody except the security team actually knew what took place in room 619, was it not possible for them to concoct a more acceptable theory as to how Biko received his brain injury? The story of the 'scuffle' is riddled with inconsistencies and the evidence was often contradictory; it would seem fairly simple to produce a more credible account of what happened.

The answer to this question only emerges after putting together the evidence of the security men, the doctors who attended Biko, and the evidence of the post-mortem. But it forms a focal-point for the whole Biko story.

The Hunger Strike

The story of the hunger-strike, false as it was, was obviously a cover-up, stated Kentridge. There were two questions that arose: Where did the cover-up start and how high did it go?

'The answers to these questions will tell us a great deal about what really happened to Steve Biko while in the custody of the security police'.

The magistrate refused to allow the Minister of Police, Mr. Kruger, to be called as a witness as to who gave him the information. Goosen, the only source of official communication from security police in Port Elizabeth, denied ever telling his superiors that Biko had threatened a hunger strike and did not know on what the Minister based his statements.

Biko died on 12 September.

On 13 September, Kruger issued his first statement, saying Biko was arrested on 18 August and from 5 September refused meals and threatened a hunger-strike, and that he had still not eaten by 11 September.

On that same day 13 September, pathologists conducted the post-mortem, and it was clear Biko had suffered extensive brain damage.

On 14 September, when Kruger kept delegates at the National Party Congress roaring with laughter at his quips about South Africa being a democratic country where prisoners had the right to starve themselves to death, *he was already in possession of the pathologists' report.*

He repeated the statement about a hunger-strike the next day, 15 September, even embellishing it: 'and indeed, he began to push away his food and water that were continually given him so that he would freely eat and drink'.

On that day Dr. van Zyl, who examined Biko the day he died, signed a statement saying he had been told Biko had refused to take food or liquid for a week, which was why he had been given a vitamin injection and intravenous drip.

On 16 September, four days after his first statement, the Minister denied suggesting Biko had starved himself to death. 'I gave categorically the fact that he had gone on hunger-strike. That was given to me by the police'.

On 7 October, Kruger brought an urgent Press Council action against the *Rand Daily Mail* over a report headlined: 'No sign of hunger strike—Biko doctors'. The Press Council upheld Kruger's complaint and reprimanded the *Mail* for 'tendentious reporting'.[35]

In the 17 October edition of *Time* magazine (long after the post-mortem results were publicly known) Kruger again said: 'He refused to eat. Those were the facts I gave . . . *He had definitely gone on a hunger strike. There is a medical history about that*'.

More than five weeks later, Kruger made the first reference to a possible 'struggle' between Biko and the police. On 23 October in an interview with the *New York Times*, Kruger said: 'There may be evidence of a struggle and things like that . . . I mean there were struggles that would probably come out . . . This follows automatically from an arrest with a stroppy person'.

Finally, in the week the inquest began—and 8 weeks after Biko's death—Kruger confirmed to foreign correspondents that Biko had died of head injuries. Asked to explain, he said: 'I can explain that by saying it doesn't seem to be any

119

evidence at all of any police involvements and a man can damage his brain in many ways. I can tell you that under Press harassment I've often felt like banging my head against a wall too, but realising now, with the Biko autopsy, that it might be fatal, I haven't done it'.[36]

The hunger-strike story evidently originated from the Port Elizabeth Security Police delivering Biko to Pretoria, and was conveyed verbally through warders to the Pretoria doctor who gave Biko the intravenous drip and who was probably asked to report to security head office in Pretoria as to the cause of death. What is important is not so much the origin of the story as the way in which Kruger persisted with it long after it was patently false.

Kruger colluded with the police in spreading a false cover-up story, and then persisted in it. At first it was part of a general concealment of the truth. It was persisted with when vital medical evidence had not yet been made public. It reveals with great clarity the extent of a cover-up, originating in a police department, propagated from the highest office, and never subsequently rescinded by the Minister of Police. The cover-up was assisted by the Magistrate who refused to let it be investigated and left it to stand unchallenged and uninvestigated by police or justice personnel even when totally refuted.

Kruger did not apologise for his part. Why should he? It is however, a vital pointer to understanding other seemingly contradictory features of the behaviour of those in authority.

The Naked Man

Why naked? Biko was kept totally naked for the first 20 days; permitted to wear shirt and trousers when removed from Walmer jail to room 619; left naked again (and chained and manacled) on the floor of the interrogation room; taken naked on the 11-hour night drive to Pretoria . . .

Was he kept naked to humiliate him? Kentridge asked Sergt. van Vuuren, the warder at Walmer police station. 'I cannot say', the warder replied—he was acting on instructions from Colonel Goosen.

Why was Biko kept naked in Walmer police cells? Kentridge asked Major Snyman. Snyman replied that he was acting on instructions given to prevent a recurrence of suicide in police cells.

Why the leg irons?

It was the custom, Snyman said.

Why was Biko kept naked? Kentridge asked Colonel Goosen.

There was a clear pattern of suicide among detainees, the Colonel replied, so everything with which detainees could hurt themselves, including clothes, were taken away.

'I myself am totally unconvinced by this explanation' writes Sir David Napley, 'which I believe to be both implausible and inconsistent with the rest of the police evidence which portrays Mr. Biko as aggressive, intractable and unco-operative.

'There was, I believe, a more convincing, albeit Machiavellian reason for Mr.

120

Biko's naked state. It was of a piece of what was aptly called 'the callous treatment' meted out to him by the security policy which has shocked world opinion..
'The totality of the conduct of the security police seems to me to fit in with an approach to, and a pattern of, interrogation which has certainly not been peculiar to the security police at Port Elizabeth ... The magistrate could have taken notice of the fact that the lowering and breaking of the spirit by such means, where it is intended to subject a person to interrogation, is a well-documented course open to those who are prepared to stoop to the employment of such treatment.... The time arrives when it is believed that the prisoner has been suitably conditioned and violence is applied before the actual interrogation begins or during the course of it . . . The circumstantial evidence leads inexorably to this conclusion'. (It should be noted that no evidence was ever given to show that Biko's spirit was broken, despite his treatment. On the contrary, police statements of his 'aggressiveness' during interrogation on the 6th indicate this was not so.)

Biko wrote that Black Consciousness brings group pride and the determination of the black to rise and attain the envisaged self. 'Freedom is the ability to define oneself with one's own possibilities held back not by the power of other people over one but only by one's relationship to God and to natural surroundings'. Biko's philosophy challenged not only the economic power of the whites, but white culture and white religion—and most of all, the status of whites, a position of absolute power and believed superiority enhanced by tradition, by laws and by religion. 'The black man sees himself as being complete in himself', he wrote. 'It makes him less dependent and more free to express his manhood. At the end of it all he cannot tolerate attempts by anyone to dwarf the significance of his manhood'.[37]

But nor could the whites tolerate him becoming a man. For white South Africans, being a man means first and foremost superiority over the blacks. But what if the black finds in his turn that his manhood depends on equality with the white? It is then that the white begins to feel his very existence diminished and cheapened. It is not only the economic consequences of emancipation that appal him, but the implied threat to his own status as a human being.[38]

Steve Biko's challenge to the whites was not simply to their power, but also to a system of beliefs around which white lives are constructed. He pointed out that, whatever its economic origins, 'after generations of exploitation white people on the whole have come to believe in the inferiority of the black man, so much that while the race problem started as an off-shoot of the economic greed exhibited by white people, it has now become a serious problem on its own. White people now despise the black people, not because they need to reinforce their attitude and so justify their position of privilege but simply because they actually believe that black is inferior and bad. This is the basis upon which whites are working in South Africa, and it is what makes South African society racist'.

That racism has been institutionalised so that it is presented as an accepted way of life. Blacks must be denied any opportunity of accidentally proving their equality with whites. Hence job reservation, lack of opportunities for skilled

work, restricted entry into the professions, and at the basis, Bantu Education.
'It is not enough for whites to be on the offensive. So immersed are they in prejudice that they do not believe that blacks can formulate their thoughts without white guidance and trusteeship. Thus, even those whites who see much wrong with the system make it their business to control the response of the blacks to the provocation'. Liberals, few as they are, determine not only the *modus operandi* of those blacks who oppose the system in which they themselves are deeply involved, but also help to perpetuate the system.

'To us it seems that their role spells out the totality of the white power structure—the fact that though whites are our problem, it is still other whites who want to tell us how to deal with that problem'.[39]

Naked and chained, Biko was already reduced and rendered dependent; already, even before the interrogation and the bullying assaults, put lower down on the rung of humanity purely by virtue of physical factors. Finally he was reduced to the status of the dependent infant, incontinent, incoherent. What did it matter to them that now they could never try him for being a 'terrorist'? That is not really what they wanted. What secrets could they have prised out, had the interrogation been able to continue, had the blows to his head in those first vital seconds not proved so fatal? There were no secrets, other than the truths which he and others all down the years have tried in their many ways to present, truths openly proclaimed until their mouths were stopped, in organisations openly formed, until they were declared illegal.

In his devastating book on Auschwitz, Primo Levi writes of the meaning of being deprived of one's clothes, of even the smallest personal possessions that even a poor beggar owns: a handkerchief, an old letter, the photo of a cherished person.

'These things are part of us, almost like limbs of our body; nor is it conceivable that we can be deprived of them in our world, for we immediately find others to substitute the old ones, other objects which are ours in their personification and evocation of our memories.

'Imagine now a man who is deprived of everyone he loves, and at the same time of his house, his habits, his clothes, in short of everything he possesses; he will be a hollow man, reduced to suffering and needs, forgetful of dignity and restraint, for he who loses all often easily loses himself. He will be a man whose life or death can be lightly decided with no sense of human affinity . . .'[40]

Walmer jail and room 619 were not Auschwitz. But they were on the same road. And Biko was such a man, reduced to suffering and needs, whose death could indeed occur lightly, with no sense of human affinity.

The Bath Incident

When Biko was taken to the Sydenham prison hospital for a lumbar puncture, he was already at a stage when his mental and physical abilities were seriously impaired and rapidly declining. He could not walk by himself—possibly could not even stand alone. Yet some time in the night he is said to have got out of bed; found his clothes (surely they were not lying folded ready for him!); dressed himself; walked to the room where there was a bath; turned on the taps, filled the bath, then climbed into it with his clothes on.

This incident took place at 3 a.m., and was repeated again a few hours later, although this time the bath was empty. (Had he gone back to bed in wet clothes? If not, who changed him?)

There is nothing in the evidence that helps to make sense of this incident; but possible explanations present themselves. When Goosen suggested that Biko might have damaged his brain at this time he may not yet have heard the expert evidence concerning the time of the injury. But this suggestion may just be a pointer to what really took place. Did the security men go to the prison hospital that night? Night interrogations are their speciality—was this a last attempt to see if Biko would talk? Was it hoped that cold water would rouse him —or that he might be found drowned? This is speculation based on what is known of the behaviour of those concerned. Like the blister on his toe (when he had not worn shoes nor exercised for three weeks) no firm conclusion can be reached, but suspicions remain.

The Journey to Pretoria

A crisis faced the security police in Port Elizabeth when they received the news that Biko, summarily removed from the prison hospital, had been found lying on the cell floor in a collapsed condition, with foam on his lips.

Up to this time they had succeeded in preventing news of his condition from reaching anyone outside the club of conspirators, a club that included the doctors who had seen him and prison authorities through whose hands he had passed.

Although prison regulations require that the close relatives of a prisoner must be informed immediately in cases of serious illness, the main concern was that nobody should know (hence the falsification of his name).

Obviously the security police knew of the outcry there would be if it became known that Steve Biko had been beaten up and was brain-damaged. If he died, the storm could be faced after suitable arrangements had been made to conceal the true facts of his death. But it must be stated that there was not at this stage, nor was there at any stage, any attempt to arrange medical treatment for Steve Biko. The doctors' role was to find out what was wrong—not to recommend treatment. Finally, when they were in possession of irrefutable evidence of brain damage (there were four definite signs: the plantar reflex; the blood in the spinal fluid; partial paralysis of the left side; and echolalia, the repetition of the last word spoken to him over and over again) even then their concern was not that he should receive any treatment, but that he should be removed from hospital as speedily as possible before he was seen by anyone who might recognise him. In agreeing to his removal, Dr. Hersch had added that he should be under constant observation. Dr. Lang had not even bothered to go and see him again, until the final emergency arose.

So the problem now was not of how or where Biko could get the best medical assistance. He could not be left in the prison in his condition. To send him to one of Port Elizabeth's hospitals would risk news of his condition leaking out before they were ready. There was one solution left: to send him to headquarters in Pretoria. This would have two advantages—removing him from Port Elizabeth, where he was well known and the political atmosphere already explosive (on 30 August school students had held a memorial meeting for a student killed by police in 1976, which was broken up by the police with many arrests) and delivering him to Pretoria, where the security police were experts at concealing the truth about detainees' deaths.

This is why he was taken to Pretoria. This is why no medical records accompanied him, and none of the doctors phoned through to Pretoria prison hospital to report their findings. This is why he could be taken 740 miles in the back of a van; there was no hurry; they waited until night so that nobody would see him; they did not bother to obtain a mattress—a felt mat would do. This is why nothing went with him except a tin of water, never proffered. This is why they loaded him into the van naked and manacled and left him lying like that when they stopped to relieve themselves, and to have a joke with fellow policemen at the stations where they went for petrol.

These facts must be taken into consideration when reading through the evidence of Wilken and Goosen and Snyman on 'shamming' and giving Biko the finest medical treatment. They were all in possession of the precise facts about the blows to his head and subsequent decline. They had only one reason for that journey.

Steve Biko was sent to Pretoria to die.

Why the Police did not present a more credible story

The clue to the extraordinarily contradictory evidence presented by the police in their affidavits and in court is to be found in Dr. Lang's evidence when he stated that he had examined Biko 'as the result of a request from Col. Goosen' and had found no evidence of any abnormality or pathology.

Biko was assaulted during the night of the 6th or the early morning of the 7th September. He was struck several blows—on the ribs, twice on his lips, and blows to his forehead that rendered him unconcious. Colonel Goosen was called in and informed of what had taken place. The police now had two alternatives:

● they could state that Biko had been hit on the forehead; or

● they could deny absolutely that he had received a blow to his forehead whilst he was in room 619.

Goosen chose the second alternative. He called in his friend, district surgeon Dr. Lang (and he could not, in his evidence, state why he actually called for

124

Lang) and he asked him to make out the certificate stating nothing was wrong with Biko. To do this Lang had to ignore the lip injury, the bruised rib, the swollen hands, feet and ankles, and the wound on Biko's forehead. One wonders if he actually saw Biko.

Thus, if Biko were to suffer any after-effects from the assault, it would be possible for the police to state categorically that any marks or injuries were not sustained in room 619. The Lang certificates proved this.

But the injuries *were* sustained in room 619, and there was still anxiety that information might leak out about Biko's condition. Hence from that moment Biko was scarcely out of the hands of the security men (which incidentally makes the bath incident even stranger). He was kept in the interrogation office. When he had to go for a lumbar puncture, he was only moved after dark. His spinal fluid was sent for analysis under a false name. Goosen said, 'I had no reason to hide him'—but he *was* hidden, brought back at night from the hospital, sent to Pretoria after dark.

Despite all these precautions, the police at that stage were not in possession of two vital pieces of medical evidence. The first pinpointed the time that Biko received the head injury fairly precisely, and put it *within the hours that Biko was in room* 619. This was not disputed by any of the experts. The second concerned the period of unconsciousness that must have followed the injury.

The medical evidence proved that Biko was brain-damaged whilst in the charge of the interrogation squad; and that they must have seen him unconscious. But they already had Lang's certificate that stated nothing was wrong, so it was impossible for them now to say that Biko had bumped his head—even accidentally. Without Lang's certificate they might have said Biko tripped and hit his head against a filing cabinet; or seized a chair and was knocked on the head with it when they wrestled with him. But the mark on the forehead did not exist—Lang could not see it, nor could anyone else. The period of unconsciousness did not exist—no one had acknowledged it. So they had to deny everything, deny the blows, deny the head injury, deny concern about its seriousness.

Lang's certificate is like the missing piece of a jig-saw puzzle. Once it is put into place, those portions of police testimony and behaviour that have not been satisfactorily explained now become a clear part of the whole picture. That certificate, too hastily obtained as a cover-up, became the exposé.

In the end, nothing but the truth is plausible, and the truth was denied.

Why the Inquest?

The answer here is quite clear. South African law requires an inquest to be held when someone dies from other than natural causes. In other cases of detainees' deaths, magistrates have from time to time stated that death was from natural causes, therefore no inquest was held. In this case it was not possible to do so.

The inquest had to take place because of the two-faced nature of South African society. The face turned towards the world says 'We are a democratic country in which the rule of law prevails'. The second face, turned inwards, says 'The special branch is above the law. When law interferes with us, no rules prevail except our own. We don't work to statutes'.

Once the inquest had opened, most of the evidence could not be suppressed save by over-riding the 'public' face which was now the focus of world interest.

But what did it matter in the end ? The verdict was assured. Those in authority might have preferred to keep the details out of the press, but they did not really care. When the government press said 'This must not happen again' they were not referring to Biko's treatment but to the damaging exposure of police methods. Public face or not, it seems unlikely such an inquest will ever be held again.

Their arrogance is justified. They have the last word. But in the final analysis, what of the courts ? Do they still present a brake on police power ?

XIII

The Courts

In any society where courts exist they tend to play a significant role in the system of domination. They normally claim a monopoly of the right to sanction the use of force, and they speak in the name of the sovereign, usually on behalf of the community . . . A test frequently adopted is whether or not a legal system operates according to the Rule of Law, a concept easier to extol than to define . . . The actual effects of the legal system and the interest promoted or suppressed by it should be as much a matter for enquiry as its formal elegance or procedural equity. The enhancement of techniques to serve ends which are unjust promotes rather than reduces injustice. In this connection it should be noted that the courts give a sense of orderliness and regularity to domination.[41]

There are certain things about the death of Biko, declared the SABC, official voice of South Africa, which should be pointed out:

No one in his right mind can cast any doubt over the manner in which the inquest was conducted. It was held in open court and demonstrated the openness of the South African legal system in action . . . There are few countries, in the West even, where the security police would have been subjected to such an interrogation in open court. South Africa should be proud of this . . .[42]

There is a long standing belief that the South African legal system retains its dignity and its decency in an otherwise flawed system. While a never-ending stream of political trials pass through the courts, while defendants complain unheeded of brutality and torture, while detainees die, often unlike Steve Biko in a deep obscurity, the courts are supposed to be the bastions of impartiality and of justice.

An independent judiciary is one that functions where the rule of law exists and protects human rights South African judges rarely protect human rights. The very existence of the procedures and practices in the Terrorism Act and other repressive legislation undermines the rule of the judiciary and obstructs defence attorneys. The courts in South Africa are a part of that closed circuit of power that maintains white supremacy. During a period of many years in which apartheid laws have been consolidated and extended the ability of the courts to offer any protection against unbridled persecution and cruelty by the authorities has dwindled and vanished.

Consider the legislation that permits the detention of individuals for varying lengths of time without charging them in a court of law or allowing them any contact with family, legal advisers or independent medical attention.

● The General Laws Amendment Act, No. 62 of 1966, empowers a senior police officer to detain any person he considers suspect in terms of the Act without a warrant for a period of 14 days.

● The Terrorism Act, No. 83 of 1967, as shown on page 18 allows for indefinite incommunicado detention for interrogation.

● The Internal Security Act, No. 44 of 1950, amended in 1976 provides for two categories of detention: preventive detention and detention of witnesses.

● The Criminal Procedure Act, No. 51 of 1977, also provides for the detention of witnesses.

Experience both inside South Africa and in other countries has demonstrated that legislation of this kind has only one purpose: to allow police unfettered action, that is torture, of those detained.

Security detention is used against a wide range of individuals and groups who are not involved in activities which could in any way be labelled subversive or illegal. The Minister of Police revealed in September 1977 that since June 1976, 2,430 people had been detained. 1,307 were ultimately released without any charges having been brought against them.[43]

According to the SA Institute of Race Relations:

Large numbers of those who openly voice their opposition to the government have been detained in the past and are in detention at present. This type of action, together with other intimidating action undertaken by the police, will no doubt result in extra-parliamentary political action becoming less overt and increasingly covert. It is essential to acknowledge that structures are not provided for the majority of the population to express their political aspirations . . . The use of detention to silence dissidents, works contrary to the principle of mediation.[44]

Since 1976 school pupils constitute a large proportion of those detained. They are held, but not brought to trial.

English-type court procedures were introduced into South Africa early in the 19th century and laid the foundations for the modern court system. The formal equality of all before the courts was recognised, and the rules of evidence and procedure were modelled on those existing in England. The need to reconcile the theory of judicial equality with the practice of race inequality gave the legal system a contradictory character that persists to this day. On the one hand the courts provided a forum where the poor and dominated could seek redress of grievances in an atmosphere of decorum; on the other they furnished the machinery for the massive suppression and punishment of persons threatening the peace and property of the dominant community. 'South African courts have been by no means unique in serving these two apparently contradictory ends, but they have done so to a degree probably without modern parallel'.[45]

The majority of South Africans are black, but the courts are presided over by white judges and white magistrates, administered by white prosecutors; white attorneys and senior counsel appear together with all the white police, warders, security men, clerks. All these officials live under laws and conditions which are totally different from those of black defendants who appear in the courts. Few, if any, of the whites have even the remotest conception of what it is like to live as a black person in South Africa.

The problems and difficulties, the poverty and restrictions, the harassments, the miseries of migrant labour, the forced separation of husbands and wives, the loneliness and bleakness of life in the reserves—'Bantustans'—whose men work for those whites, far from their own wives and children, in white homes, in white-owned mines, factories, shops, offices; these are observed by very few whites. To observe leads to realisation of the necessity of change . . .

The role of the courts, theoretically, is to sit in judgment on those charged with contravening the laws of the land. Who made those laws? Who enforces them? Who must judge whom?

The judges are not directly responsible for the laws the white parliament passes (except in the sense that the whites are the voters, and therefore they participated in making that parliament). They acknowledge that their responsibility is that of pronouncing on the law rather than making it; that they must give effect to the will of parliament as expressed in the legislation. But despite that, they are capable of some effect in the way the law is administered, particularly by their own interpretations of passages in the statute that are not absolutely explicit.

For the past fourteen years, judges sitting in political trials have listened to defendants describing brutality and torture at the hands of the security police. Some judges have commented on the evidence, some have said that there should be a further inquiry into the allegations, some have simply ignored them, and some have said it is a pack of lies invented by the defendants. But whatever their attitude, none of them have let the evidence of torture influence the final verdict which is made according to laws under which the defendant has been charged.

Not one of them, not all the great body of evidence, has brought about any modification of the conditions under which detainees are held; any changes in the laws; any punishment or action against the security force. Imam Haron died with bruises all over his body and many other injuries. The police said he fell down a few stairs. The Attorney-General said an inquiry disclosed no evidence whatever which could serve as a basis for prosecution of any person.

A 69-year-old detainee, Marks Monokgotla, after terrible beatings and electric torture, managed to get a statement to lawyers and an interim five-day order restraining the police from interviewing him. A lawyer submitted the restraint on the police should be extended. This is what the judge said:

If your man is a terrorist, then the police have every right to arrest him. Don't expect me to make an order on baseless allegations. The allegations made by him are denied by several policemen. Why must I cast this terrible slur on the police? [46]

A doctor in East London testified that Washington Bongco had been admitted to hospital with numerous injuries, both ears haemorrhaging, bruises around the neck, badly swollen eyes. Another doctor said the detailed hospital records had been 'mislaid' and that the injuries were consistent with the police statement that Bongco had fallen and been in a struggle with the police during an escape bid. The judges found that Bongco's case was 'riddled with inconsistencies . . . Allegations of being assaulted were sheer fantasy. By the clearest evidence his story was shown to be untrue'.[47]

In the SASO/BPC trial in 1976 the judge ruled that denials of assault made by the security police were to be accepted by the court and that there was no evidence of physical violence involved in police interrogations of detained State witnesses.

A case as equally alarming as Biko's, where the judicial investigation proceeded further, was the Mdluli case.

On 19 March, 1976, a 50-year-old man, Joseph Mdluli, died in security police custody in Durban within 24 hours of his detention. He had been an ANC member until the organisation was banned in 1960.

Two days after his death a post-mortem examination was held from which a private pathologist retained by the family was excluded. The family lawyer, Mr. G. Mxenge, demanded that a second post mortem be held. This was refused. On 24 March Mxenge was himself detained.

Mrs. Mdluli remained adamant in her demands for a full investigation. On 12 April the Minister of Justice denied that there was any attempt to cover up the death of Mdluli.

Then on 13 May the ANC released photographs of Mdluli's corpse at a press conference in London and charged that he had been tortured to death. The photographs showed extensive injuries subsequently found to include a fractured cartilage and severe bruising to the neck, extensive bruising on the forehead, temporal area and back of the scalp, abrasions in numerous places, deep bruising near the rib cage, three broken ribs and numerous bruises and abrasions on the body and limbs. The brain was congested with haemorrhages although the skull was still intact. The lungs were blood congested and waterlogged.

In an unprecedented move on 11 June, following international protest, the Minister of Justice announced that four Security Branch policemen were to be charged with the culpable homicide of Joseph Mdluli. The trial that followed proved farcical and merely continued to conceal the responsibility for Mdluli's murder.

The four accused policemen, Captain D. F. van Zyl, Lieutenant A. R. Taylor, Detective Sergeants M. P. Makhanya and Z. Ngobese, did not even give evidence. Instead the prosecutor produced an agreed statement of facts, thus avoiding a potentially revealing cross-examination of the accused. According to the police explanation, Mdluli was arrested on 18 March at about 10 p.m. and attempted to escape from the Durban Security Branch headquarters at 10 a.m. the following morning, was restrained and a fierce struggle ensued. After the struggle Mdluli was calm and made no complaint of any injuries. This incident was reported to Major Coetzee who satisfied himself that Mdluli was not injured. Mdluli's interrogation continued with occasional breaks until about 8.30 p.m., when he suddenly got up, held his head, staggered and, complaining of dizziness, fell with his chest or neck on to the back of the chair. The chair toppled and Mdluli fell against the door. Shortly after this, at 9.55 p.m. he was dead.

This explanation could not begin to explain the extensive injuries found on Mdluli. Giving evidence, state pathologist Dr. van Straaten said that he was called to Fisher Street at about 11 p.m. and shown the body of Mdluli covered by a blanket. Photographs were taken and Dr. van Straaten examined the body shortly after midnight. An officer demonstrated to him how Mdluli had fallen over and died, although he made no mention of Mdluli hitting a chair. Dr. van Straaten stated that his first reaction on examining the corpse was 'here is a man who could have been dead for anything up to 12 hours. I did not take the body temperature as there was the cream of police society telling me that the man had collapsed and died in their presence'.[48]

When Dr. van Straaten conducted the post-mortem, he found numerous injuries which could not be accounted for by a single fall on top of a chair. He found that there had been more than one application of force to the area of the neck on which the fatal injuries appeared. Professor I. Gordon, the chief state pathologist in Durbin, corroborated Dr. van Straaten's evidence. He examined the body on 22 March at the request of Dr. van Straaten, who pointed out his findings. They decided to change the description of the cause of death from strangulation to 'the application of force to the neck'. He confirmed all the injuries and said, 'it seems that the application of blunt force took place at separate times and not in continuity'.

Acquitting the accused, Mr. Justice James found that the case against the four policemen had not been proved. 'If police evidence was to be accepted at face value the four accused were not reponsible for the death of Mr. Mdluli . . . it was clear from the doctor's evidence that Mr. Mdluli died almost immediately after receiving the neck injuries. If he had died of these injuries in the morning after a scuffle with the four accused, all the policemen in the building would have had to enter an elaborate conspiracy to conceal his death until evening. I consider the probabilities overwhelming that the accused did not give Mdluli the fatal injuries to his neck that morning. As this was the only occasion on which it is alleged that they assaulted Mdluli, it follows that they were not responsible for his death. It then follows that whatever view one may take of what occurred, all the accused are entitled to an acquittal on the charge they face'.[49]

The carefully constructed prosecution case provided the four accused with alternative ways out. By alleging that Mdluli had died only late in the evening the four accused could avoid being found guilty of the charges because the prosecutor specifically charged that Mdluli had died in the morning. If they were found guilty it would have been on the basis of the admission of a scuffle taking place in the morning, in which case they could claim to have inadvertently killed Mdluli whilst attempting to restrain him. The judge could not accept that a whole building full of police could conspire to conceal the circumstances of

Mdluli's death. Dr. van Straaten had neglected to take the body temperature and therefore could not be sure of the time of death. The clear evidence of Mdluli's widespread injuries could not however be reconciled with the police explanation. The judge found their story open to 'very considerable doubts'. He concluded 'I need hardly say that the problem of how Mdluli met his death is one that should be solved and it is one of great importance'.

These remarks absolve the judge of any responsibility and refer investigation of the death back to the police. In February, 1977, the Natal Attorney-General announced that the investigation into the death of Joseph Mdluli, ordered by Justice James, had been completed. No new evidence had come to light, he said, and no further prosecutions would take place.

Joseph Mdluli was listed as a co-conspirator in the marathon trial in Pietermaritzburg of ten men charged with ANC activities held from May 1976 to July 1977. The judge in the trial, Mr. Justice Howard, dismissed the testimony of the accused that they were tortured, but in a section of his 15-hour judgement stated that the injuries that caused Mdluli's death in detention could not have been self-inflicted nor caused accidentally. The judge found that most, if not all, of the injuries on him were inflicted by one or more unidentified members of the Security Police. 'We are satisfied that Mr. Mdluli sustained the injuries while he was in the custody of the Security Police. There is no evidence of how he suffered the injuries or in what circumstances. That is a matter peculiarly within the knowledge of the persons in whose custody he was at the time and none of them has given evidence', said the judge.[50]

No further action was taken by the Attorney-General.

And suppose the judicial system were to accept evidence of torture. If, after prolonged detention under Section 6, when the victim is finally charged and has access to a lawyer, he attempts to obtain an interdict to restrain the police from further violent interrogation, the state will simply withdraw the charges and put the victim back again under Section 6, where he is held totally incommunicado. And further, if a judge actually dismisses charges against the defendants—as has happened from time to time where the case has been too obviously full of flaws, or state witnesses have refused to testify when brought to court—then the defendants are simply re-arrested before they leave the dock and held once more in total inaccessibility by the security police under Section 6.

The main criticism which could perhaps be advanced in relation to the conduct of most of the judges is not so much that they help to enforce race discrimination because they are corrupt, cowed or consciously biased, but that they do so willingly; not that they lack courtesy or decorum, but that they use polite and elegant language to lend dignity to laws which impose segregation and harshly penalise radical opponents of a system of government almost universally condemned. Instead of investing their office with the prestige associated with the pursuit of justice, they allow the prestige associated with their office to be used for the pursuit of injustice.[51]

The Biko inquest played an important part in maintaining the myth of the independence, detachment and impartiality of the South African courts. Every single participant in an inquest of this kind becomes in one way or another an actor playing a part from which he can deviate only a little. The court is a masquerade. The decision has been taken before the court sits. It is a conspiracy of which the very highest, the Minister of Police and Justice himself, J. Kruger, and the lowest, policemen, warders or clerks are a part.

With notable exceptions, South Africa's lawyers as a whole and the organised legal profession have done little to mitigate the crudities of the Terrorism Act, whose very purpose is to obtain evidence by the use of torture. Even where the lawyers are wholly concerned with the experiences of their defendants, they have to make difficult decisions. As an eminent jurist observed of one of the earliest Terrorism Act trials: 'The reality of prison torture contrasts with the inadvisability of registering such a complaint. It was generally agreed that to complain about torture in the setting of the terrorism trial would inflame the prosecution and the judge. It was not in the best interests of the defendants, who were on trial for their lives, to assume this risk in an atmosphere such as prevails in South Africa'.[52]

Lawyers appearing for defendants at these trials, or for the families of murdered men at the inquest, know that the Terrorism Act is the very negation of justice. But the state prosecutors, the attorneys-general, the magistrates, the judges—they are also familiar with the law and the general trend in the laws. We don't make the laws, say the legal men; our job is to apply them, to see they are adhered to. From where comes that potent echo from the past? When is the stage reached when we are no longer dealing with the nicety of jurisprudence but with the essential quality and survival of justice itself?

Where inquest magistrates are concerned, there is little attempt at a display of judicial erudition. In the Biko case this was particularly obvious. Prins only intervened to ask questions suggesting a partiality towards the police. He gave Kentridge some freedom in cross-examining police and doctors on their contradictory statements and affidavits. *But the outcome had already been decided.* The Attorneys-General for the Eastern Cape, and for the Transvaal, both stated before the inquest even began that no criminal proceedings would be instituted.

Undoubtedly all witnesses experienced some uncomfortable moments in the dock, and were totally unable to answer some questions. But they could maintain their arrogance, nor need they feel any twinges of conscience or regret. They knew nothing would happen to them. Why should it? They were protected by that closed circuit of power from Kruger—Minister of *Police, Justice* and *Prisons*—down to the newest warder or hospital orderly, which maintains the apartheid state.

When counsel for Biko's family finished the drama with his trenchant, direct, unanswerable accusations, the show was over. It was not necessary for Magistrate Prins to do any more than say, symbolically, 'The End'. Thus his insultingly-brief findings; no reasons were necessary; no reprimand to those in high places who had lied and lied; no word of regret.

133

The courts remain, but there is no rule of law. The security police are totally above the law. There are no laws nor rules of conduct to which they adhere; there is no court to which, ultimately, they must be answerable. They are now invested with power and secret invulnerability that places them in a position that is unassailable. No more is a court decision final or binding. If a judge, confronted with a patent lack of evidence, finds the political defendant 'not guilty', there are the sinister men of the 'special branch'—the security police—who step forward once again. Theirs is the ultimate authority.

XIV

Postscript

From the time that Steve Biko entered room 619 in Sanlam Buildings, his destiny was sealed. On the morning of 7 September, twenty-four hours after his interrogation began, the blows were inflicted. The man who had laughed at danger and provocation, who had formed organisations and edited magazines, who had argued and debated and propounded strong ideas, no longer existed. His past life had been sheared away. What was left was the frame of Steve Biko, enclosing now only a suffering mutely and inadequately expressed and callously ignored.

In the next few days he groped through the haze and pain of his obliterated reason for the receding world. The doctors came and went and came again. Perhaps less is expected of the police, who after all are dedicated to uphold the immoral laws of the apartheid state. But what of the doctors and the Hippocratic Oath? If only one of them had, by voice or gesture, shown care, concern, understanding, for the suffering of this human being, this fellowman, whose life was so rapidly flowing away, he would have redeemed himself. But no; they all condemned him to the total isolation and loneliness in which he moved through incomprehension and darkness to his death.

He who would not give in
Has been done to death
He who was done to death
Would not give in.

The warner's mouth
Is stopped with earth
The bloody adventure
Begins;
Over the grave of one who loved peace
Slog the battalions.

When he who did not fight alone is done to death
The enemy
Has not yet won.

Bertolt Brecht

135

References

The extracts from the inquest proceedings are taken from the *Rand Daily Mail* which published extensive and largely verbatim reports often running to several pages following each day's court proceedings. Sir David Napley's report is given in its entirety in Appendix A.

1. *Sunday Times* (London) 18.9.77
2. *Times*, 12.1.77
3. Quoted in *Sunday Times*, 18.9.77
4. *Rand Daily Mail*, 14.7.77
5. *Rand Daily Mail*, 17.9.77
6. Reprinted by the UN Centre Against Apartheid, in Document 9.77
7. Reprinted in Karis and Carter (eds.) *Documents of African Politics in South Africa*, (1973) Vol. 2
8. *ibid.*
9. *Second Report of Arrests, Detentions and Trials of Members and Supporters of the Various Black Consciousness Movements*, quoted in UN Document 9.77
10. Poems quoted in *Black Theatre*, IDAF Fact Paper No. 2, June 1976
11. quoted in *Sechaba*, Vol. 7. No. 1.
12. quoted in *African Communist*, No. 51
13. This and subsequent quotations are from Biko's contribution to *Black Theology: The South African Voice* ed. Basil Moore, reprinted in *Times* 23.11.77
14. see note 6
15. SASO/BPC trial account in UN Document 9.77
16. Verbatim translated transcript from tape-recording of the account of the imprisonment and death of Steve Biko, given to the Transvaal Congress of the Nationalist Party on 14 September, reprinted in *Rand Daily Mail* 16.9.77
17. Reprinted in translation in *Cape Times* 16.9.77
18. Monitored by the BBC *Survey of World Broadcasts*, 19.9.77
19. Reprinted in *Cape Times*, 15.9.77
20. *Cape Times*, 16.9.77
21. *Star*, 22.10.77
22. *New York Times*, 26.9.77
23. *Rand Daily Mail*, 19.9.77
24. *Evening Standard*, 20.10.77
25. *Rand Daily Mail*, 10.11.77
26. *Sunday Times* (Johannesburg) 19.11.77
27. *Cape Times*, 4.9.76
28. Quoted by pathologist Prof. Loubser later in the proceedings.
29. *Times*, 18.11.77
30. *Times*, 1.12.77
31. *Guardian*, 3.12.77
32. *Sunday Times* (Johannesburg) 4.12.77
33. SABC 5.12.77, monitored by BBC *Survey of World Broadcasts*.
34. *New Statesman* 9.12.77
35. *Cape Times*, 8.10.77
36. *Rand Daily Mail*, 7.11.77
37. see note 13.
38. This concept is advanced by Jean-Paul Sartre in his preface to Henri Alleg's *The Question*.
39. see note 13.
40. Primo Levi *If This Is A Man*.
41. Albie Sachs, *Justice in South Africa* (1971)
42. SABC 5.12.77, monitored by BBC *Survey of World Broadcasts*.
43. *Rand Daily Mail* 2.9.77
44. S.A. Institute of Race Relations, *Report on Detentions Without Trial* 1967-77.
45. Sachs, op. cit.
46. *Terrorism of Torture* (IDAF, 1971)
47. *ibid.*
48. *Natal Mercury*, 27.10.76
49. *Rand Daily Mail*, 29.10.76
50. *Rand Daily Mail*, 26.7.77
51. Sachs, op. cit.
52. Prof. Richard A. Falk, Professor of International Law at University of Princeton USA, who attended the trial of 35 Namibians in 1968 on behalf of the International Commission of Jurists.

Appendix A

Report by Sir David Napley, British Law Society, invited as independent observer by The Association of Law Societies in South Africa.

Stephen Biko Inquest

1. I was invited by the Association of Law Societies of South Africa to attend as an independent observer at the inquest into the death of Mr. Steve Biko. I attended the hearings at the Old Synagogue in Pretoria from the 17th November, 1977 until the 2nd December, 1977. I was not able to be present during the first three days of the hearing due to commitments in England. However, I fully familiarised myself with the proceedings over those three days from the Court records.

2. The evidence was adduced partly in English and partly in Afrikaans. In relation to the latter, I had through the good offices of the Transvaal Law Society been provided each day with assistance from a practising attorney who translated the Afrikaans evidence into English for me as the Inquest proceeded.

3. The proceedings have been widely reported throughout South Africa and indeed the World, and I therefore consider it unnecessary to review the whole of the evidence placed before the Chief Magistrate, Mr. M. J. Prins who sat with two assessors, Professor I. Gordon and Professor A. Olivier.

4. I would wish to place on record that I was greatly assisted, particularly in relation to the evidence given in Afrikaans and in checking my own notes of the proceedings (in advance of receiving each day the record of the Court record for the previous day) by the reports, which appeared daily in the *Rand Daily Mail*, which displayed a high degree of accuracy, comprehensiveness and objectivity.

5. Upon my arrival in South Africa I was virtually unfamiliar with both the law and procedure of the South African legal system. It follows that in observing the Inquest I had, of necessity, to use as the yardstick against which to base my opinion, my experiences of the English legal system over the last 45 years. In doing so I made allowance for variations between the English and South African systems.

6. I was concerned whether the inquest was conducted with thoroughness and fairness. I am abundantly satisfied that insofar as the South African Government was concerned, the fullest possible inquiry was facilitated from the moment that the Inquest began.

7. I am unable to express the same view concerning the investigation by the Police Department which preceded the Inquest. This appeared to me to have been perfunctory in the extreme. The death of anyone whilst detained in the custody of security police demands rigorous investigation. The death of this particular detainee rendered it manifest from an early date that it was an especially sensitive area for the South African Government in relation to World opinion. The inquest revealed, for example, that the officers closely concerned with the custody and interrogation of the deceased at the relevant time were questioned by means of roneoed forms, which contained a series of questions with alternative answers. They were required to strike out the reply which they considered inappropriate to their answers. Vital documents such as a significant telex and a bedside medical record, were only discovered as the Inquest proceeded, and then only by reason of the diligence of Counsel appearing for the relatives of the deceased. It is clear that an investigation conducted by experienced police officers with a little of the enthusiasm and vigour with which they customarily appear to question detainees would have elicited the truth from the security police in far less time than was necessary to demonstrate their mendacity in the witness box, as, in my opinion occurred. Moreover, if at the outset of the Inquest it had been possible for the Deputy Attorney-General to announce the findings of such

137

an investigation and the fact that appropriate action was to follow, much of the opprobrium which has now ensued would have been avoided. In my opinion the failure of the police properly to investigate this matter served a grave disservice to the Government which employed them, to the cause of Justice and to the police force itself. However, it was evident to me that the Chief Magistrate was concerned to ensure that the enquiry extended over every relative facet. Indeed, there were some aspects of which it may be said that far more time was devoted to it than was justified.

8. I am in full accord with the finding of the Magistrate that Mr. Biko died as result of a head injury associated with extensive brain damage and resulting complications. I also wholly accept that on the evidence adduced before the Magistrate he had no alternative but to find in relation to the verdicts open to him under Section 16 of the Inquests Act that he could not, on the evidence available, determine that death was brought about by an act or omission involving an offence on the part of *any person*, i.e. any particular person. On the principle that in an Act the singular also includes the plural, this would also be true in respect of any *particular persons*. I do not, however, apprehend on a strict reading of Section 16 that it would have been irregular for the Magistrate to have found that the death was caused by one or more of a group of persons without specifying such persons with particularity. In my opinion, however, he was demonstrably wrong in adding the rider that the head injuries which resulted in death, were probably sustained in a 'scuffle' with the police at police headquarters.

9. It has unfortunately become a matter of international speculation as to why the Magistrate did not give his reasons for his decision, particularly since he took some trouble to give his reasons on each occasion when ruling on the admissibility of evidence. It is perhaps both fair and germane to observe that whilst I largely disagree with his rulings on these matters, I am satisfied beyond any doubt that he was not influenced by any consideration other than, within the limits of his legal knowledge, to conduct the Inquest in a fair, open and unrestricted fashion. For the uninformed it should be pointed out that Magistrates in South Africa are not appointed from the body of practising lawyers. They are drawn from the ranks of civil servants; they generally have no legal professional qualification and accordingly lack grounding in legal principles and practice. It is a matter of surprise to me that more use is not made in South Africa in its magisterial system of the wealth of untapped legal talent in both branches of the legal profession.

10. Since I disagree with the Magistrate and consider he could, and should, have reached a different conclusion in that regard, it is just and proper that I should not follow his regrettable example by failing to set out the reasons for my view. Accordingly, I now propose to present them.

I.   The late Mr. Steven Biko was stopped on the 18th August, 1977 at a road block set up by Lt. Oosthuizen of the security police GrahamsTown, since he suspected that Mr. Biko was concerned in the distribution of inflammatory pamphlets. It was common ground throughout the Inquest that Mr. Biko was at that time a strong and healthy man; twenty six days later he was dead as result of brain injuries.

II.   On the 19th August, 1977, he was delivered into the custody of the Security Police, under the command of Col. Goosen at Port Elizabeth and detained under the Terrorism Act No. 83/67.

This Act is designed 'to prohibit terroristic activities' and is drawn in wide terms, of which a relevant example found in Section 2 of the Act (which must be read in conjunction with Section 2(1)) is the fact that it is Terrorism 'to cause, encourage or further feelings of hostility between the white and other inhabitants of the Republic . . . with intent to endanger the maintenance of law and order in the Republic or any portion thereof'. It is no part of my function, intention or desire to involve myself in the internal political problems of South Africa which are rather more difficult to solve than international politicians and armchair critics might have us believe. Suffice it for me to observe, particularly since it bears upon the opinion which I have formed, that these provisions are wide enough to encompass detention without any limitations as to the period of detention: without any provisions that the detainees must (if at all) be prosecuted within a stipulated time or released, and by Section 6 (5) of the Act no court of law shall pronounce upon the validity of any action taken under the Section (which facilitates the detention) or order the release of any detainees. While expressing therefore no view upon the wisdom of the Act having been drawn in such wide terms, or as to the fact that international opinion might consider that it reflects little confidence being placed by the Government in the judiciary whose wisdom and judgment it excludes, it was nevertheless by virtue of these provisions that the police acted in detaining Mr. Biko.

III. In an affidavit of the 20 October, 1977, sworn by Lt. Kuhn of the South African police he stated that he visited Mr. Biko in his cell at 8.10 p.m. on the 22 August, 1977 and on 8, 9 and 10 September. In a later affidavit dated the 9 November, he admitted that he had been wrong in stating that he so visited on the 8, 9 and 10 September. However, if as the witness explained, this was a mere mistake, it is pertinent to observe that it was only one of a number of examples where deponents to affidavits appeared to have testified under oath in a somewhat cavalier manner, to put it at its lowest. Certainly, this fact does not appear to have ruffled the imperturbability of those senior police officers charged with the responsibility of investigating the conduct of those serving under them.

IV. It was testified by a number of witnesses in oral and affidavit testimony that when asked if he had any complaints, Mr. Biko never registered any. It was also suggested to the district surgeons in a series of leading questions put by counsel representing the police and accepted by them, that at no time did Mr. Biko make any complaints as to his treatment or of any assault. It was reminiscent of the armed forces where officers enquired of other ranks whether they had any complaints in relation to their food. It used to be cynically observed that they were always free to complain so long as they did not mind being put on a charge.

In my view the fact that the detainee failed to make any complaint when invited to do so or that he failed to complain to a doctor employed by the State, at a time when he was held, incommunicado, under callous and degrading conditions by the security police is of no evidential value whatsoever and is no more than one of many debating points made in answer to the case advanced by Mr. Biko's relatives.

V. During part of his detention Mr. Biko was kept naked, although under constant surveillance by the security police. This was common ground. The justification for this was said to be to prevent him from committing suicide. I myself am wholly unconvinced by this explanation which I believe to be both implausible and inconsistent with the rest of the police evidence which portrays Mr. Biko as aggressive, intractable and uncooperative. There was, I believe, a more convincing, albeit Machiavellian reason for Mr. Biko's naked state. It was of a piece with what was aptly called 'the callous treatment' meted out to him by the Security Police which has shocked world opinion and the vast bulk of South Africans themselves. It is unnecessary to recount all the details. However, even before the alleged fight with the police, Mr. Biko had been manacled by the hands and a foot; had been left in that condition through the night of the 6 September; had been provided only with a mat on which to lie; and had for part of the time been left only with trousers which were soaked in urine; had been left on a cell mat and with blankets in a similar condition; had been denied exercise outside his cell, etc., etc. I apprehended in the course of the evidence produced at the trial, that, in particular, depriving him of clothes and refusing him the opportunity to purchase food from outside the prison were contrary to the terms of the warrant of arrest under which he was held, and there is reason to believe there were a number of other serious violations of prison regulations by the Security Police.

VI. The totality of the conduct of the Security Police seems to me to fit in with an approach to, and a pattern of, interrogation which has certainly not been peculiar to the Security Police at Port Elizabeth. Although specific evidence was not led at the inquest in this regard, the Magistrate could have taken Judicial notice of the fact that the lowering and breaking of the spirit by such means, where it is intended to subject a person to interrogation, is a well documented course open to those who are prepared to stoop to the employment of such treatment. One need do no more than refer to the work of William Sargant, M.A., M.B. Cantab., F.R.C.P., F.R.C. Pschy. D.P.M. sometime Honorary Consulting Psychiatrist and Physician in charge of the Department of Psychological Medicine, St. Thomas's Hospital, London, England, in his book 'The Battle for the Mind'. Just as police excesses and abuses of police power are not peculiar to South Africa, so there is no reason to believe that that which, however regrettably, occurs elsewhere is alien to the South African Security Police. Thus, it is by no means unknown, that the time arrives when it is believed that the prisoner has been suitably conditioned and violence is applied before the actual interrogation begins or during the course of it. The prisoner is then told in the police vernacular of the country concerned 'now if you do not want some more of that, start to sing'. It must be said that there was no direct evidence whatsoever adduced that this occurred, but in my opinion the circumstantial evidence, as I believe I can demonstrate, leads inexorably to this conclusion.

VII. Mr. Biko was detained on the 18 August, 1977. His interrogation was commenced on the 6 September, 1977. If the police can be believed, the delay of 20 days before questioning him was because they desired first to question those detained with him. It is equally consistent with the process of 'conditioning'. During the whole of that time he was held incommunicado; he must have known of the anxieties of his family as to what had become of him. He was deprived of his clothes; he was refused access to food of his own choice at his own expense. He was denied normal exercise. On the 6 of September he was interrogated, with a mid-term break, from 10.40 hours to 1800 hours according to the affidavit of Major Snyman, the Officer in charge of the interrogation. Five officers were allocated to the interrogation so that while Mr. Biko could not rest, they could be working in shifts. That night he was left naked in an office as his cell, with a mat on which to sleep, with his hands handcuffed and one foot manacled to an iron grille.

If one accepts, as I do, that this reflects a classical example of systematic brutalisation and degradation designed to soften up for interrogation, why should one resist the inference that the final factor must have been omitted, namely the application of violence? There is less reason, as will appear, for rejecting this inference when one considers the remaining evidence and in particular, the medical evidence.

The only other relevant factor is whether despite the virtually irresistible circumstantial evidence, one can accept the police account as one of truth. I was not present to observe the police evidence given on the first three days. I have, however, read the record and was not impressed. I was, however, able to observe the demeanour in the witness box of Colonel Goosen, the Officer in charge of the Security Police; of Lt. Wilken, who was said to be guarding Mr. Biko on the vital night of the 6 September and of Warrant Officer Fouche. I was quite unable to accept them as witnesses of truth. The record which sets out the able cross-examination by Mr. Kentridge, S. C., on behalf of the relatives abundantly demonstrates this fact. It was doubly evident when they were observed.

Lt. Wilken, on entering the Court presented an air of amiability to all concerned, and spent some time smiling. At one point, when his face was turned from the Magistrate and he became put out by a reference by Mr. Kentridge to his having played the part of a night nurse, he revealed, when taken off his guard, a picture, to which his eyes gave testimony, of underlying anger and a degree of viciousness which I personally found to be terrifying.

VIII. Police evidence asserted:
   a. that Mr. Biko was given meals of soup, magou (i.e. magewu) bread, margarine, jam, coffee and water;
   b. that he refused the soup and magou and the bread heaped up in the cell; according to a statement made by a visiting Magistrate who saw Mr. Biko on 2 September he was told by Mr. Biko: 'I only live on bread here' and 'I want to be allowed to buy food'. The Magistrate's statement stood unchallenged at the Inquest. It was suggested in the course of the police evidence that they believed, at least in the early stages, that Mr. Biko was on a hunger strike, and certainly prior to the time when he sustained the injury which led to his death. No enquiry was pursued at any stage of the proceedings as to whether it was evident to them that Mr. Biko's refusal to eat the food was not an act of defiance but was conditioned by the belief in consonance with his statement to the Magistrate, that he did not eat the food because he found it unpalatable, and hoped that by rejecting the food provided he might still be allowed to purchase food from the outside. One cannot exclude the suspicion that the police, if questioned, may have been able to throw more light on this aspect than they vouchsafed.

IX. On the 6 September, 1977 at about 10.30 hours Mr. Biko was taken to the offices at Sanlam Building for interrogation by Major Snyman and his team of interrogators. They were five in number, namely Major Snyman, Captain Siebert, Warrant Officers Marx and Beneke and Detective Sergeant Nieuwoudt.

X. On the medical evidence it was common ground that:
   a. Mr. Biko had suffered at least three brain lesions occasioned by application of force to his head, and

b.   that he suffered his brain injury between the night of the 6 September and 7.30 a.m. on the 7 September.

As to point (b) I am of the view, however, that the time when the injury had been sustained is far more likely to be not later than 0715 hours on the morning of 7 September, rather than 0730 hours.

The giving of the latest time at which the injury could be sustained rests primarily on the evidence of the police that he was interrogated from 1040 hours on the 6 September until 1800 hours on that day. During that time, they said, he was not only alert, but aggressive, although later he became more 'co-operative'. I can find no reason why this part of the police evidence should be untrue; indeed, the medical evidence lends verisimilitude to it. It was only on the following morning after the interrogation had been resumed that Colonel Goosen, Head of the Security Police, Port Elizabeth, urgently summoned a doctor. Moreover, the medical evidence aroused no doubt that, to put it at its lowest, the symptoms which occasioned the summoning of such medical assistance were fully consistent with an application of force to the head which would have occurred at a time comparatively soon before the symptoms appeared. As to the latest time at which the injury could have been sustained, the evidence of Major Snyman, who was in charge of the interrogation, was that he came on duty with his team at 0700 hours on the 7th. Regrettably, no one, including, in this connexion, counsel for the relatives, subjected the police to close questioning in relation to the timing of events between the vital period of 0630 hours to 0730 hours. Thus it is not unreasonable to assume if the officers came on duty at 0700 hours that there would be some lapse of time before the actual interrogation was resumed. Indeed, there is some corroboration in the evidence of one officer that it commenced at 0715 hours. According to the evidence of Major Snyman, he gave instructions for the removal of the manacles from Mr. Biko's hands and feet. This too must have taken a little time. He then asked him if he had any complaints. It then appeared from the evidence of all the officers that this was almost immediately followed by a violent attack by the deceased. After he had been brought under restraint and manacled, Major Snyman discontinued the interrogation and made a full oral report to Colonel Goosen, who had arrived at approximately 0730 hours.

This strongly indicates to me:

a.   that the interrogation was not in any meaningful way resumed, and
b.   that the display of violence took place almost at the same time as the endeavour was made to resume the interrogation.

This is of special significance when, as will later appear, one considers the uncontradicted medical evidence that the brain injury that the deceased received is normally followed by the violence, symptoms and conduct which the police and the doctors described; particularly if he had sustained the brain injury shortly before the attempted resumption of the interrogation.

XI.   The cause of death being undisputed, the only question remaining for the Magistrate was whether the death was brought about by an act or omission on the part of any person as provided in Section 16(2) of the Inquests Act.

XII.   No direct evidence was at any time adduced from the police as to any application of force to the head of the deceased, which could have caused such an injury to the brain. Such half hearted attempts as were made were consistent only with a blow to the back of his head as he fell. The injury causing death, or at least, the vital injury was to his left forehead.

XIII.   Three theories were advanced as to how the brain injury may have been sustained:

a.   that it was self-inflicted; the medical evidence was unanimous that it was not a case of self-inflicted brain injury; this was certainly not the case in the light of the extent of the injury found here. There was no evidence adduced in relation to the general behaviour of the deceased which, in my opinion, gave any credence to this suggestion. The Doctors were also unanimous that they had never heard of a self-inflicted brain injury in their experience, and knew of no recorded instances in the text books. I personally rejected it as wholly implausible.
b.   that the deceased sustained the injury in the course of the 'scuffle' which occurred when the interrogation was resumed some time after 0700 hours on the 7 September. The Magistrate in giving his decision stated that it was probably during the course of this scuffle that the injury was sustained. According to the testimony of the

141

police, directly after resuming the interrogation on that morning they confronted the deceased with information which had been learnt from Mr. Biko's associates, whereupon it was said that he threw a chair at Major Snyman. The deceased, said the police, had a wild expression in his eyes. He charged Warrant Officer Beneke, slinging wild blows at him and pinning him against a steel cabinet. Major Snyman and Captain Siebert went to Beneke's rescue and tried to hold Mr. Biko. Whilst wrestling they bumped into tables and chairs. The other officers hearing the noise from an adjoining room entered and five policemen brought Mr. Biko under control by pinning him to the floor, where handcuffs and feet shackles were applied. If this struggle was the occasion for the brain injury in the course of falling about, it is strange that the police sustained no injuries at all, save that one officer had a bruise on his elbow which on one occasion he said was to his right elbow and on another occasion he said was to his left. When Colonel Goosen was fetched to Room 619 where the deceased was detained, he, Mr. Biko, still had a wild look in his eyes and a visible swelling to his upper lip. He spoke incoherently and in a slurred way and with a heavy tongue and Colonel Goosen accordingly summoned the District Surgeon.

XIV. According to a statement made by Dr. Lang, Colonel Goosen expressed concern to him at 0930 hours on the 7 September, that Mr. Biko might have suffered a stroke since he was neither eating nor able to speak and he was not using his limbs. Although Dr. Lang did not find paralysis of the limbs, there is no reason to doubt, assuming Dr. Lang's assessment is correct, that some time prior to 0930 hours and subsequent to 0730 hours an evident inability to use the limbs had been noted by Colonel Goosen, particularly since, he, as a layman, thought Mr. Biko had had a stroke. It is also significant that although Dr. Lang found no organic cause, he did remark upon Mr. Biko's weakness in his legs.

XV. During the course of the Inquest much time was devoted to consideration of highly skilled and expert medical evidence. The bulk of it was devoted to the solution of three main questions:

i.   whether the ultimate death of Mr. Biko was attributable to negligence on the part of the district surgeons.
ii. whether Mr. Biko's brain injuries, and particularly the three lesions were attributable to one or more blows.
iii. whether injuries such as Mr. Biko sustained may have involved a period of unconsciousness and if so, for how long?

The first point was clearly relevant for the Magistrate but was quite peripheral to the principal issue. Suffice it to say for my purpose that both the Government of South Africa and the Medical Authorities have much to consider and rectify arising out of the conduct of the District Surgeons in this matter.

As to point ii, in his final submission, Mr. Kentridge on behalf of the family, indicated that he did not feel on the evidence that he could ask the Magistrate to reach a finding as to whether the brain injuries were occasioned by one or more blows.

Counsel for the police asserted that this amounted to an abandonment by Mr. Kentridge of that part of his case. That was, of course, wholly incorrect. Mr. Kentridge was, in my view, quite right under the circumstances. There was a sharp conflict of views as to whether one or more blows occasioned the brain damage. Whilst on a balance of probabilities, I would personally have preferred the view that there was more than one blow in that connection it could not wholly be removed from the sphere of speculation. Acceptance of the fact that more than one blow occasioned it would have lent great weight to Mr. Kentridge's contentions, but the absence of such a finding, did not materially weaken the totality of his contentions. In any event it was common ground that there were at least two blows, one to the forehead and another over the lip.

As to iii there was complete unanimity amongst the medical witnesses that it was inconceivable that Mr. Biko, after sustaining injuries of the sort disclosed, could not have suffered a period of unconsciousness from 10 minutes to one hour. Counsel for the police took refuge in the fact that there was not 100% certainty in the evidence as to unconsciousness, since the experts conceded that, although unlikely, they could not wholly exclude the possibility that unconsciousness did not ensue. He further argued that it would be unfair, under those circumstances, to infer that unconsciousness was present. With respect to Counsel for the police, I consider this argument unrealistic. As the doctors pointed out, within the field of medicine it can rarely be asserted that any diagnosis or conclusion can

142

be arrived at on a basis of 100% certainty. I was left in no doubt that unconsciousness must be assumed to have occurred. I am certainly satisfied that no British jury, properly directed, would have had any doubt and I have reason to believe that any British or South African High Court Judge of experience would have had any doubt that the doctors were right in saying that it was inconceivable that unconsciousness did not ensue and that the alternate possibility was so remote in the circumstances as to be unworthy of weight or credence.

XVI.   I had the impression that when the Magistrate (as I believe, by misdirecting himself on the law) refused permission for Brigadier Zietsman to be called as a witness, he had not appreciated that it would remain open to Mr. Kentridge to cross examine Colonel Goosen as to the information contained in the Brigadier's affidavit. Had he done so, I suspect that he might not have excluded the Brigadier's evidence. What emerged, as a consequence of this cross examination, was that a telex had been sent on 16 September over the signature of Colonel Goosen to the Security Police Headquarters in Pretoria which referred to an injury 'which was inflicted' on Mr. Biko at 0700 hours on 7 September. Moreover, as Mr. Kentridge pointed out in his final address a vital point in the telex which the witnesses in their evidence had failed to disclose was that Mr. Biko's inability to speak was directly related to the injuries inflicted.

XVII.   It was for all practical purposes common ground that at almost every opportunity Colonel Goosen endeavoured to convey to the doctors the fact that Mr. Biko was shamming. Colonel Goosen was, however, on the horns of a dilemma: if he was telling the truth when he said no improper pressure was put on Mr. Biko, the inevitable conclusion was that there was nothing about which Mr. Biko needed to sham. He had only to say that he did not wish to answer. If, per contra, he was shamming serious illness then the only reason for doing so was to avoid treatment to which he knew he was to be subjected or had already been subjected, to compel him to speak. Whichever way Colonel Goosen prefers to have it he fails. A further indication of the unreliability of Colonel Goosen's evidence was illustrated by Mr. Kentridge. The Colonel endeavoured to maintain his belief that Mr. Biko was shamming and that he was in ignorance as to how serious was his condition. He maintained that the purpose in sending him to Pretoria was to enable proper medical assessment to be made as to whether he was shamming or not. In the light of Colonel Goosen's statement that he made endeavours to obtain a military aircraft as a matter of urgency to fly Mr. Biko to Pretoria solely to ascertain whether he was shamming, one cannot long hesitate before wholly rejecting this explanation. If he was shamming what was the urgency? Still another indication of Colonel Goosen's unreliability is the fact that in the telex to which reference is made above, Mr. Biko was described as having been, at the time when he was despatched, in a 'semi coma'. This was never previously revealed in evidence and was utterly at variance with Colonel Goosen's statements on oath that he did not believe Mr. Biko was at that time seriously ill.

XVIII.   If the medical evidence is considered in isolation one might well come to the conclusion that whilst Mr. Biko had died as result of a blow or blows to his head resulting in brain damage which caused death, it would, however, be unsafe to draw any further inference in the light of the conflicting expert medical views. However, one cannot and must not look at that evidence in isolation; it must be evaluated in conjunction with the totality of the evidence. Due to my absence on the first three days I was not able to see some of the police officers give evidence; I have, however, read the record. It cannot be fair to put it any higher than that I was not impressed with their evidence. I did, however, have the opportunity of seeing Colonel Goosen and Lieutenant Wilken, and observing their demeanour, in the witness box. In my opinion it was impossible to accept them as witnesses of truth, nor would in my opinion, any experienced lawyer or as I have already observed, a British jury. Still another feature of Colonel Goosen's testimony which is decisive to my mind is that whether one rejected his repeated protestations, both in evidence and in his statement to the doctors that he thought Mr. Biko was shamming, as I do, or accepts it, one asks oneself why someone with his intelligence did not place in the forefront of the information he imparted to the doctors the fact that Mr. Biko had most probably sustained an injury to his head? This is particularly so, since he said he had the possibility in mind at the time. If he was honest when he said that he believed that the only circumstances known to him under which the deceased could have sustained the injury were those which he described in relation to the so called 'scuffle' on the 7 September, it follows that he had absolutely nothing whatsoever to hide. Why did he so strongly stress that Mr. Biko was shamming and studiously avoid bringing the head injury to the notice of the doctors concerned? To me this affords the strongest possible indication, verging upon certainty, that there was some happening which he was anxious to hide. Once one is satisfied, about that, as I am, it can only be that he knew the injury did not result from an accident. On the medical evidence he must have known that Mr. Biko had been unconscious, when that occurred and why. It was more than a Freudian slip that the telex which was belatedly uncovered, disclosed a blow having been 'inflicted' on Mr. Biko on the morning of the 7th.

XIX.   There was common agreement amongst the medical experts as to the likely clinical symptoms which result from brain lesions such as those suffered by Mr. Biko.

Professor Loubser, who was called by the Deputy Attorney-General agreed that the description of symptoms contained in a chapter of a book called 'Injuries of the Brain and Spinal Chord and their Coverings' by Sir Charles Symons, reflected a striking resemblance between Sir Charles Symons' graphic description and some aspects of the evidence. Professor Gordon, one of the assessors, described Sir Charles Symons as one of the greatest neurologists to have practised in the United Kingdom this century.

It is necessary to compare this account with the behaviour of Mr. Biko as revealed in evidence.

As we have seen, he would first be rendered unconscious for anything from 10 minutes to one hour. As he comes round he would be 'unaware of his environment and be inaccessible'. 'He is at first mute, unresponsive to commands and inert'. 'Later he begins to be restless and while still mute and stuperous may become restive and violent'. Is it not therefore a strong possibility that his violence at the time of the so called scuffle was not the occasion of brain injury, but the result of one already sustained? Immediately before, according to Major Snyman, he had been unresponsive, and then had 'a wild look in his eyes' and 'was slinging wild blows'. If it took five men to restrain him was this not itself a manifestation of the state of his mind? Moreover, although it is unnecessary to pursue the whole course here the later symptoms are equally consistent. A confused state 'when the patient gets out of bed, puts on his clothes and runs away' is also consistent with the deceased having been found twice in a bath of water wearing clothes. Moreover, there is sometimes a temporary return to a greater or less degree of rationality which could coincide with the time when Dr. Lang saw him and found him able to speak and walk, although weak in his limbs.

XX.   As indicated the explanation offered for the violence is the evidence of the police that it was prompted by the disclosure of certain information to Mr. Biko which had been revealed by his associate in detention. This, however, raises so many improbabilities as to render it quite unacceptable to me. The police assert that the reason for the delay in interrogating Mr. Biko, for some 20 days was whilst they interrogated his fellow detainees. Thus, such information as they had received was in their possession on the 6 September when he was interrogated from 1040 hours to 1800 hours. Why did they not produce that information over that long period? They seemed to have got nowhere; and if, however, they did produce it, why did he become violent concerning something which he heard the previous day without becoming violent?

Moreover, was such violence, even for such a reason, the reaction of a normal man? What was he to gain by it? No one suggested anything. If it was unrestrained anger no evidence suggested that his temperament normally manifested that trait. Again, one is drawn to the conclusion that the outburst was a result of the injury and not the occasion of it.

XXI.   It is, in my opinion, reasonable to postulate as follows: The purpose of Mr. Biko's detention was to obtain information concerning alleged terrorist activities. A recognised course for eliciting information is to condition a person, e.g., by holding him incommunicado for 20 days, subjecting him to hardship and deprivation such as that endured by Mr. Biko. Not long before the interrogation was to be resumed at 0715 hours on the morning of 7 September, he sustained an injury which proved fatal, and that injury was inflicted by one or more persons with a view to rendering him compliant.

In summary the following salient facts emerged:

1.   The dishonesty of the police in stressing to the Doctors that Mr. Biko was shamming illness and the fact that they steadfastly failed even to suggest to the Doctors that he sustained a blow to his head, abundantly demonstrates that they had something discreditable to hide.

2. The fact that Mr. Biko must have had a period of unconsciousness before 7.15 a.m. on the morning of the 7 September must have pinpointed the onset of the brain damage and the way in which it was sustained.

3. The failure by the police to mount and pursue a meaningful and vigorous investigation prior to the Inquest as to the full and true circumstances was, and could only be, attributable to a significant reluctance to uncover the truth.

4. The demonstrable pattern of conditioning of the deceased for interrogation renders it improbable, in the face of the callousness involved throughout, that actual violence would have been abhorrent and absent.

5. The medical evidence established that the onset of the brain damage was at least as consistent with a blow having been received prior to 0715 hours on the 7 September, as in the 'scuffle' at about that time.

6. The oral evidence of the police was unconvincing and for the most part probatively unacceptable.

7. The police, in whose custody the deceased had been when he was held incommunicado, advanced no explanation as to how he could have sustained a blow to his forehead, consistent with the brain damage subsequently disclosed.

In short, I was left in no doubt that Mr. Biko died as a result of brain injury inflicted on him by one or more unidentified members of the Security Police at some time prior to and reasonably proximate to 0715 hours on the morning of the 7 September, 1977. A blow or blows no doubt intended only to hurt, caused brain damage which resulted in death. If, within the first few hours of sustaining the injury, the full and true facts had been given to the Doctors, and they had been allowed to place Mr. Biko in a provincial hospital, with all the advantages of the excellent and experienced medical services available in South Africa, Mr. Biko might still be alive. After the first few hours, as the Autopsy and the medical evidence showed, the resultant damage became irreversible.

11. Although the Magistrate clearly did all in his power to ensure that all such available evidence as he believed relevant, was placed before him, the real circumstances relating to Mr. Biko's injury and death had never been fully investigated by the police. In England perhaps fortuitously, there is at the moment a clear advantage to be enjoyed in relation to enquiries concerning abuses by the police. England has a number of separate and distinct police forces. It is customary for an enquiry into one police force to be conducted by officers of another. This reduces the opportunity for the particular force under enquiry to close its ranks. Having regard to both the rivalry and pride which exists in the individual forces this usually results in the enquiry by the officers being conducted with no less, and sometimes more vigour, than was the case when investigating crime believed to have been committed by a citizen. South Africa has only one national police force and one can see the difficulty of securing an investigation of the kind which would be possible if separate forces existed. Moreover, the Security Police, which is only a branch of the State police force, appears to be given a degree of licence which is unwarranted. They appear to regard themselves as above the law, exercising wide discretionary powers and Colonel Goosen in evidence virtually said as much. It is for others to consider how these difficulties might be overcome, if, as I hope and believe is the case, those on whom the responsibility rests, are anxious to ensure that there is no repetition of the unhappy story of Mr. Steve Biko. It may be worth the Government considering the establishment of some special branch similar to the A10 Branch set up in England by Sir Robert Mark, when Commissioner of Police for the Metropolis, for the avowed purpose of monitoring the Force and thus ensuring the most diligent and searching enquiry where it is necessary.

Certainly there appears today to remain a strong case for the fullest independent investigation by specially selected police officers into the causes of this unhappy death.

12. Apart from the above there are other matters which those responsible may feel need consideration. There was in my opinion a prima facie case of obstructing the Course of Justice. I am not, however, an authority on South African Law and those who are may wish to give consideration to it. Such limited research as I have been able to undertake indicates, as stated in Vol. 2 of Hunt on S.A. Criminal Law and Procedure on Page 144: 'In most cases X knows that proceedings are pending or that investigations are taking place with a view to possible prosecutions but it is sufficient if before either stage is reached X commits his actus reus in order perhaps to forestall all possible investigations'. The authority relied upon is State V. Neethling 1956 (2) S.A. 165(0) at 168.

Colonel Goosen asserted that he was anxious Mr. Biko should not die; he had good reason. One would therefore have expected as I have previously indicated that he would have vouchsafed the information to the doctors. I was personally left in no doubt that the reasons why this was not done was to avoid drawing attention to the real cause of the injury and resultant proceedings. It must have been known to the police officers concerned that if the whole of the facts had been disclosed, there was a probability almost to the point of certainty, that such proceedings would follow. (b) It is also for consideration whether there is not evidence that several members of the Security Force agreed expressly or by implication to frustrate a proper investigation in order to avoid the inevitable consequence of a trial. If that was so there was a conspiracy and anyone who later joined in it would have been equally guilty.

13. There is a further aspect which I believe calls for investigation. Counsel representing the police appeared on the instructions of the State Attorney. He (the State Attorney) similarly instructed both counsel for the doctors and the prisons. The latter in this context need not be further considered since it was common ground that no allegation was made against the Prisons.

From the outset, and before the enquiry began, it must have been evident and thus clearly predictable that the case for the doctors was that if they had been negligent in diagnosis, this was due to the failure of the police to give them adequate information as to the behaviour of the deceased and of the treatment to which he had been subjected. It was the case for the police, however, that they subjected the deceased to the hardship which he endured, including their failure to make provision for proper hospital treatment, only because of wrong diagnosis by the doctors. If this is not a case of conflicting interests it is difficult to know where a stronger example could be found. The matter was further complicated by the fact that Dr. Hersch, who was not a State employee, was also represented by the same Counsel as represented the other doctors. There was also a manifest conflict of interest between them. The district surgeons contended that any failure on their part to take proper action was attributable to the fact that Dr. Hersch failed to make clear to them that he was satisfied there was evidence of brain injury; on the other hand Dr. Hersch's case was that he had been called in as a Consultant and had indeed made his anxieties plain to the doctors; that the failure to follow his diagnosis made the responsibility theirs. This was also a predictable area of conflict. An additional factor which emerged was that when it must have been evident that an inquest would take place, Counsel instructed for the police interviewed Dr. Tucker. Someone may wish to satisfy himself that the ethical proprieties in this matter were observed. It is still true that justice should not only be done but should manifestly be seen to be done. One speculates as to how an Attorney could instruct counsel to conduct a vigorous case against another person for whom he is also acting or vice versa. Moreover, how can an advocate appear for those whose interests are diverse to others with whom he had already discussed their case. I do not agree with the apparent view of the State Attorney that joint representation was justified because both the Doctors and the police are State employed. For the Doctors more was involved here than money. There was reputation and professional status at stake.

14. The third aspect of the matter which, as it seems to me, is worthy of consideration is the situation of the Attorney-General and Deputy Attorney-General both in this matter, and generally.

As I understand the S.A. procedure: under the Inquests Act the papers are first considered by the Public Prosecutor. If he decides on the prosecution of any person responsible for the death an inquest is not held. If he does not so decide, the papers are returned to the Magistrate and an inquest is held. At the inquest the Magistrate (unlike the practice in England) may cause evidence to be led by the Public Prosecutor or anyone appointed by him. In this case the Deputy Attorney-General was nominated. At the conclusion of the inquest the record is returned to the Attorney General again to consider whether criminal proceedings shall be brought. He then decides whether or not action is to follow. In the conclusion of his final submission Mr. Kentridge commented upon the fact that the only part which the remaining counsel for the other interested parties had played in relation to the witnesses was to endeavour to repair the effect of his cross examination.

I do not personally believe that this was a justified criticism insofar as it applied to the Counsel representing the police, the doctors or the prisons. In my view their function was to protect the interests of those whom they were instructed to represent. I am much less happy about the position of the Deputy Attorney-General. It appeared to me, both

146

on a true reading of the Inquests Act and the decision in the case of Timol that it was his duty dispassionately to present to, and test, on behalf of the Magistrate, all the relevant available evidence. I may have been wrong but I came away with the clear impression that, on such occasions as he intervened, his questions were directed to preserve the position previously taken up. To this end on occasions he intervened to support the police and doctors although they were already represented by other Counsel. Whilst I am not satisfied that his presence in fact made any significant difference to the outcome of the enquiry, it seemed odd to me that the Deputy Attorney-General, having been seen to be asking questions apparently designed to sustain the earlier formed view, should later be called upon to play the decisive part in determining whether criminal proceedings should nevertheless be taken.

15. It remains only for me to say that anyone who goes to South Africa as a guest, as I did, comes away with a deep sense of appreciation for the warmth of the hospitality and the kindnesses bestowed. One also feels deeply how intractable the problems facing them appear to be. Good manners normally dictate, moreover that one should refrain from criticism. It was, however, expressly indicated to me that I was invited on the basis that I would honestly and objectively express my view. I can only hope that what I have written will cause further consideration to be given to the events which brought about the tragic and disturbing death of Mr. Biko. It was heartening to see, in most respects, the Judicial processes so greatly respected in South Africa, not least by the many able and conscientious people engaged in the administration of Justice.

The sense of outrage which appears to have been generated by this inquiry can still perhaps be assuaged, (as I and so many others would wish), if, even at this stage, proper and vigorous police enquiries are pursued, in the knowledge and to the end that those who frustrated Justice in this case performed no service to their country or to the establishment of better international relations.

SIR DAVID NAPLEY

Appendix B

Deaths in Detention under Security Legislation in South Africa

1.9.63 BELLINGTON MAMPE
Cause of death undisclosed.

5.9.63 'LOOKSMART' S. NGUDLE
Official explanation of death 'suicide by hanging'.

24.1.64 JAMES TYITYA
Official explanation of death 'suicide by hanging'.

9.9.64 SULIMAN SALOOJEE
Official explanation of death 'fell out of seventh floor window'.

7.5.65 NENGENI GAGA
Official explanation of death 'natural causes'.

8.5.65 PONGOLOSHA HOYE
Official explanation of death 'natural causes'.

1966 JAMES HAMAKWAYO
Official explanation of death 'suicide by hanging'.

9.10.66 HANGULA SHONYEKA
Official explanation of death 'suicide'.

19.11.66 LEONG YUN PIN
Official explanation of death 'suicide by hanging'.

30.11.66 AH YAN
Official explanation of death 'suicide by hanging'.

9.9.67 ALPHEUS MALIBA
Official explanation of death 'suicide by hanging'.

11.9.68 J. B. TUBAKWE
Official explanation of death 'suicide by hanging'.

date undisclosed AN UNIDENTIFIED MAN
Died at an undisclosed time of an undisclosed cause at an undisclosed place (Information given in the white parliament on 28.1.69).

5.2.69 NICHODIMUS KGOATHE
Died of broncho-pneumonia as a complication of head injuries. The police said the head injuries had been the result of a 'slip in the shower'.

28.2.69 SOLOMON MODIPANE
The cause of death was described as 'natural causes'. The police said he 'slipped on a piece of soap and fatally injured himself'.

10.3.69 JAMES LENKOE
The official explanation was 'suicide by hanging'.
Post-mortem findings were consistent with both hanging and death by electric shock including traces of copper in a wound on the toe.

1.6.69 CALEB MAYEKISO
Died of 'natural causes'.
His wife said he was healthy when taken away two weeks before his death.

16.6.69 MICHAEL SHIVUTE
The official explanation: 'suicide' on the night he was detained. There was no further explanation.

8.9.69 JACOB MONAKGOTLA
The cause of death was 'thrombosis'.

27.9.69 IMAM ABDULLAH HARON—a prominent Muslim leader.
The police said he 'slipped down the stairs'.

There has been no explanation of how he received the 27 bruises on his body.

22.1.69   **MTHAYENI CUTHSELA**
The police said 'natural causes'.
But witnesses said he was beaten frequently with sticks and given electric shocks through electrodes attached to his ears and penis.

27.10.71   **AHMED TIMOL**
Police say he 'fell from the 10th floor window at police headquarters, Johannesburg, while being interrogated'.
The inquest verdict was suicide and that he had not been tortured or assaulted before his death.

19.3.76   **JOSEPH MDLULI**
Died through the 'application of force to the neck'.
Four security police were charged with Mdluli's manslaughter and acquitted.

25.6.76   **WILLIAM TSHWANE**
Died as a result of gunshot wounds inflicted by the police. His family were not told of his death until 14.10.76.

15.7.76   **MAPETLA MOHAPI**
The cause of death was 'force applied to the neck'. The police said he had hanged himself with his jeans.

2.9.76   **LUKE MAZWEMBE**
Said to have committed suicide by hanging. The inquest adjourned indefinitely without reaching a verdict.

25.9.76   **DUMISANI MBATHA**
The police merely said that he 'became ill'. He was detained during a demonstration and died in hospital two days later.

28.9.76   **FENUEL MOGATUSI**
He officially died of an 'epileptic fit'. His family said that he had never been an epileptic.

5.10.76   **JACOB MASHABANE**
The police said he hanged himself with his shirt.

9.10.76   **EDWARD MZOLO**
'cause undisclosed'.
There has been no further explanation.

18.11.76   **ERNEST MAMASILA**
'Suicide by hanging' two days after being detained. No further details.

25.11.76   **THABO MOSALA**
'Natural causes'.
Officially explained as internal bleeding from a gastric ulcer.

11.12.76   **WELLINGTON TSHAZIBANE**
'Suicide by hanging' two days after being detained.

15.12.76   **GEORGE BOTHA**
Alleged to have committed suicide by jumping down a stairwell in Port Elizabeth security police HQ. Post mortem report showed several injuries sustained before death. The inquest found death was due to a head wound for which no one was to blame.

date undisclosed   **TWALIMFENE JOYI**
Cause of death undisclosed.

9.1.77   **NABAOTH NTSHUNTSHA**
He is said to have 'hanged himself'.
On 24.1.77, the Minister of Police said that 'unauthorised incisions had been made at the mortuary making a complete post-mortem impossible'. According to the pathologist retained by the family, there was one incision from the throat to the groin. The other was from ear to ear across the top of the skull.

9.1.77   **LAWRENCE NDZANGA**
'Natural causes'.
No further details.

20.1.77   **ELMON MALELE**
'Natural causes'.

He died in a Johannesburg hospital after a brain operation, officially from 'hypertension and spontaneous haemorrhaging'.
The inquest ruled that no one was to blame for his death.

15.2.77   MATHEWS MABELANE
Police said he fell from the 10th floor window of police headquarters in John Vorster Square during interrogation. At the inquest the judge accepted the police statement that Mabelane escaped onto the ledge and then fell accidentally.

22.2.77   SAMUEL MALINGA
'Natural causes'.
He died in hospital in Pietermaritzburg apparently from respiratory failure after a stroke sustained in police custody.

26.3.77   AARON KHOZA
He 'hanged himself'.
The inquest was told that he was found hanging from the bars of the window in his cell by a jacket and shoelaces. Doubt was cast on this, however, by photographs taken before the body was removed, showing a glassed window frame inside the bars. This would have made his hanging as the police described it impossible. When the court inspected the cell there was no glass in the window.

7.7.77   PHAKAMILA MABIJA
Police said he 'fell from a window during interrogation'.
The inquest was told that the windows, which were usually locked, had been opened to allow some fresh air in. Mabija's sister told the court a detective had told her brother 'say goodbye to your family, you will not see them again . . .'

2.8.77   ELIJAH LOZA
'Natural causes'.
The police said he died in hospital after a stroke. His daughter said when she visited him 'there were bruises and a swelling on his head and he was jerking so violently he had to be restrained. When I asked him which parts of his body were painful, he pointed to his head, shoulders and private parts'.

3.8.77   HOOSEN HAFFEJEE
He 'hanged himself'.
The official post-mortem confirmed that he hanged himself with his trousers. But an independent post-mortem showed 25 abrasions on the body, arms and legs, plus a number of burn marks.

15.8.77   BAYEMPINI MZIZI
'Hanged himself'.
No further details.

12.9.77   STEVE BIKO

Since Steve Biko's death another political detainee has died in police custody:

7.11.77   BONAVENTURA MALAZA
Police said he 'hanged himself'. No further explanation nor inquest inquiry.

It should be pointed out that the above list refers only and specifically to people detained under South Africa's *security laws*. In February 1977, The Minister of Police stated in Parliament that 130 people had died in police custody during 1976. Of these, 13 were political detainees held by the security police in incommunicado detention.

Many others have died in police custody whilst detained under non-security legislation but for political reasons. Some have simply disappeared. It is therefore difficult to arrive at an exact list of deaths in detention; the names given here represent those which can be established with certainty, but the true figure is likely to be higher.

Printed by A. G. Bishop & Sons Ltd., Orpington, Kent.

A Selected List of
DEFENCE & AID PUBLICATIONS

SOUTH AFRICA: THE IMPRISONED SOCIETY 40p
by Allen Cook (1974, 80pp)

Examines conditions in Apartheid's prisons, particularly in relation to political prisoners.
"A valuable source of information", *Time Out*.

THE SUN WILL RISE 40p
Edited by Mary Benson (rev. ed. 1976, 56pp illus.)

The major court statements of imprisoned South African leaders.

RACE AGAINST RACE 60p
by Joan Brickhill (1976, 77pp illustrated)

South Africa's "multi-national" sport fraud.

FORBIDDEN PASTURES: EDUCATION UNDER 60p APARTHEID
by Freda Troup (2nd imprint 1977, 71pp illustrated)

"First rate publication . . . excellent value . . . makes astringent and absorbing reading from start to finish as well as being an essential reference work", *Times Educational Supplement*.

ZIMBABWE: THE FACTS ABOUT RHODESIA 60p
(1977, 84pp illustrated)

Useful for the specialist, essential reading for the general reader " . . . an amazingly comprehensive book, which documents in clinical detail the measures that make up a racist State", *Catholic Herald*.

WINDOW ON SOWETO 80p
by Joyce Sikakane (1977, 80pp illustrated)

"This window will provide us with a brilliant glimpse of truth about blacks in South Africa", *Link*.

ZIMBABWE IN STRUGGLE (1978) £4

An exhibition of 80 photographs displayed on 12 posters.

AFRICAN WORKERS AND APARTHEID 50p
by David Davis (1978, 50pp)

Describes how black workers in South Africa are impoverished and oppressed by Apartheid.

Available from IDAF Publications, 104 Newgate St., London EC1A 7AP.